saturday
kitchen
suppers

saturday
kitchen
suppers

Over 100 seasonal
recipes for weekday
suppers, family
meals and dinner
party showstoppers

WEIDENFELD & NICOLSON

First published in Great Britain in 2014
by Weidenfeld & Nicolson
an imprint of Orion Publishing Group Ltd
Orion House
5 Upper St Martin's Lane
London WC2H 9EA

An Hachette UK company

10 9 8 7 6 5 4 3 2 1

ISBN: 978 0 297 86912 2

Recipes and text © Cactus TV Limited 2014 with the exception of the
following: pp. 7 © Tom Kerridge, 8 © James Martin, 15 © Gennaro
Contaldo, 53 ©Angela Hartnett, 93 © Tom Kitchin, 131 © Bryn Williams,
179 © Phil Howard, 134 and 180 © Martin Morales, 227 © Michel Roux Jr
Design and layout © Weidenfeld & Nicolson 2014
Edited by Zelda Turner and Kate Wanwimolruk
Design and art direction by Loulou Clark and Us Now
Photography by Andrew Hayes-Watkins
Food Stylists: Anna Burges-Lumsden, Lisa Harrison
Food Team: Sal Henley, Jane Brown
Prop Stylists: Tamzin Ferdinando, Loulou Clark

A CIP catalogue record for this book is available from the British Library.

Printed and bound in Italy

The Orion Publishing Group's policy is to use papers that are natural,
renewable and recyclable products and made from wood grown in
sustainable forests. The logging and manufacturing processes are
expected to conform to the environmental regulations of the country
of origin.

www.orionbooks.co.uk

**If you'd like to visit the studios, experience *Saturday Kitchen* behind
the scenes and meet chefs from the show in the Michel Roux Jr
Cookery School on site, go to www.cactuskitchens.co.uk.**

Contents

Foreword

Hooray for a new *Saturday Kitchen* cookbook: proper chef recipes, designed and written up for you to cook at home.

For me, *Saturday Kitchen* is one of the most iconic cookery shows that this country has seen. It provides that fantastic crossover from the bona fide chef world straight into the living rooms of the Great British public on a Saturday morning. It is fantastic to see chefs in normal clothes, even if it means noticing how bad Glynn Purnell's T-shirt is!

There is a real gang vibe in the studio when it comes to filming. You may not know this, but we actually do a full-scale rehearsal of the show before it is aired. Everyone arrives at the studio at 6 a.m. where the home economists, sound men and producers are already set up and ready to go. The fact that the show is live leads to a nervous anticipation, knowing that between two and three million people are about to tune in for their weekly hit of seasonal cooking and a classic Keith Floyd or some other magic snippet of cookery television from the past. As a guest chef, standing there waiting behind the stove for the show to start, I imagine the feeling is comparable to a footballer going out to play a game on a Saturday in the Premier League. No matter how many times you do the show, you still get the goose bumps and that slight sick feeling in your stomach when the intro music starts.

One particular morning stands out as a personal highlight. I was appearing on the show alongside the talented and charismatic Alex Atala from D.O.M. restaurant in Brazil, who was serving ants that tasted of lemongrass, and the hugely entertaining Warwick Davies, star of *Life's Too Short* and Harry Potter. I'm fairly certain that if you had woken up late with a hangover and just turned the television on, seeing the good-looking James Martin and the rest of us, you wouldn't be sure if it was a cookery show you were watching or something from Narnia...

This is a great selection of recipes, from some fantastic chefs. Enjoy making them all, but don't worry, none of them contain ants!

Introduction

Well, here we are. Eight years have passed since I uttered my first few mumbled lines on a Saturday morning, live to the nation. None of us working on that first broadcast could have predicted what a massive success the show would become or how long it would run for. That is testament to the great team we have behind the camera, from pot washers, runners and directors to the whole production staff. Despite the 5 a.m. starts, every one of us remains passionate about the show.

We have about eight minutes on the live show to demonstrate a stunning, tasty dish, which is achievable at home, so planning and coordination are key. Forget fancy gadgets, the studio kitchen has the same basic things you have at home – a fridge, a cooker, some quality pots and pans (ovenproof, non-stick and sturdy) and someone to do the cooking.

Admittedly the very best chefs in the world cook at our hobs, and when I'm peeling, chopping or whisking for the likes of Michel Roux, Antonio Carluccio and Pierre Koffmann, my job feels like a dream come true. I think I have the best commis chef position in the world. I don't have to go to Michelin-star restaurants to see what the top chefs are practising. I can watch their signature dishes cooked right in front of me, and ask questions (and perfect new cooking methods) along the way.

Now all these ideas and techniques are right in front of you, in this collection of our favourite, seasonal dishes from the last couple of series. Taking advantage of the extra space a book allows, the recipes come peppered with helpful tips and strategies for spending time in the kitchen more efficiently. Read through the method right to the end before you begin. Prepare the ingredients. Organise your kitchen and your equipment before the main event and you'll be a better and more relaxed cook, whether you're feeding your family or presenting your dishes live to the nation.

As for store cupboard basics, these are so important for the home cook (and make life easy). At the top of our list is cold-pressed rapeseed oil, a deliciously nutty, creamy British oil with half the saturated fat of olive oil and a very high smoke point, so you can use it for roasting or frying. Fresh herbs and chillies are cheapest when grown from seed in a windowbox and harvested as and when they are needed. Spices are the easiest way to make food exciting and flavoursome – buy these whole and lightly roast and/or grind as needed. Fill your cupboards with sea salt and whole black peppercorns, stock cubes, panko breadcrumbs, tinned tomatoes, dried pasta and shop-bought pastry.

Deciding what to cook for your *Saturday Kitchen* supper is the big challenge.
There's so much to choose from in these pages, from the simplest suppers
to show-stopping dinner party ideas, from modern British classics (from the
likes of Nathan Outlaw, Tom Kitchin and Sat Bains) to French, Italian, Indian,
South African, Latin American and Chinese-inspired dishes. The mix
is eclectic and global, but the ingredients are often British. The common
theme is seasonality. It's what excites the Saturday Kitchen brigade most:
the desire to showcase what is fresh, to cook with the best of what the
season has to offer.

I'm all for better welfare for animals as I was a pig farmer for half of my life,
so I would urge you to buy organic and free range if you can. By doing so,
we will all raise the welfare standards of food production across the UK.
Local butchers and fishmongers, although sadly a dying breed, offer the best
advice and selection when buying meat and fish and should be supported at
all costs.

From my time working on the farm, I know only too well the processes
involved in getting food to our tables and how much hard work it is to
produce just the carrots for your Sunday lunch. Supermarkets are getting
better and, if you know what to look out for, it's easy to save money and
cook well with an abundance of seasonal produce (see page 230). Internet
shopping also has its place: with the click of a mouse you can order the best
ingredients – like fresh fish direct from the coastline – straight to your door.

I hope you enjoy this book and the recipes as much as we have enjoyed
putting it together. Lastly, can I say a big thank you to all of you for watching?
You ruin my weekends – I'm knackered when I'm done! – but I love it, and the
fact that millions of you watch is the icing on the cake and for that I can't say
thank you enough.

James Martin.

Cooks' notes

The recipes in this book have been arranged by season, reflecting the kind of dishes the *Saturday Kitchen* brigade cook on our show. The mix is eclectic and global, the ingredients are not too difficult to get hold of and often British. Our focus is always on what is fresh and the best of what the season has to offer (see page 230). Vegetarian dishes, soups and starters are followed by robust main dishes featuring a fantastic variety of fish and interesting cuts of meat as well as an abundance of seasonal vegetables. The collection includes seasonal menus, sensational dinner-party fare, foodie ideas – from a gourmet Scotch egg to the latest fast-food craze, Bunny Chow – and plenty of fast, fuss-free suppers, for when you want something tasty and easy, midweek.

Eggs/butter

All eggs are medium and butter is unsalted unless otherwise stated.

Stock

Supermarkets sell good-quality stocks these days but we have also included a Make Your Own chapter (see page 207) packed with basic recipes for stocks, dressings and sauces.

Oven temperatures

We use fan-assisted ovens on the show. If you are cooking with a conventional oven (without fan assistance), follow the temperature guidelines in this book, but increase the cooking time slightly.

Conversion table

Recipes are given in metric measurements. Strictly speaking, 1 ounce equals 28 grams; in practice, we express an ounce as 25 grams. This is to make your sums a little easier: with most recipes a few grams here or there won't make any difference.

Measurements

1 tsp is the equivalent of 5ml
1 tbsp is the equivalent of 15ml

Spring

Finally, after the long sleep of the cold, bleak winter months, the days become longer and warmer and there is a feeling of activity around. I remember growing up in my village of Minori on the Amalfi coast; more people were seen out and about, and the markets and greengrocer would come alive with colour as the stalls and shop fronts filled with new produce and we enjoyed the first broad beans, peas, baby onions and carrots, asparagus, fresh borlotti beans, artichokes, spinach and endless salad leaves. It was also time to go for walks in the hills to pick wild herbs – rocket, fennel, dandelion, garlic, chicory, nettles, sorrel; not forgetting sweet, delicate *fragoline di bosco* (wild strawberries).

I still enjoy collecting wild herbs in England and do so each year. I was also so pleased to discover a type of edible mushroom growing in parks and meadows here known as the St George because it usually appears around 23rd April. This mushroom has a fresh, almost grass-like flavour to it and I love to combine it with wild garlic tagliatelle – spring on a plate!

For me, each new ingredient means a new dish and a celebration. These days we are able to find all sorts of produce all year round, but I still love to wait for each new season for fresh, local produce wherever I am in the world – you can't beat the taste, freshness and value for money of eating seasonally.

Spring has everything to look forward to – warmer weather, its food and its celebrations. With the warmer and longer days, I used to spend more time by the sea and go fishing. The fishermen could be seen on the beach mending their boats and nets in preparation for the new season's catch, which would swim nearer our shores – it was time for sea bream, octopus, sea bass and anchovies.

We looked forward to succulent spring baby lamb, goat and chicken. Lamb or goat was a must for our Easter lunch, which we would enjoy with fresh peas. Eggs tasted amazing at this time of year as hens spent more time outside and supplemented their diet with young green shoots – they were so fresh I used to eat eggs raw, beaten with a little sugar!

I love spring and love appearing on *Saturday Kitchen* – in fact, when I am invited to cook on the show it feels so spring-like every time, no matter which time of the year it might be – so warm, so rejuvenating, so much fun and always a foodie celebration!

Gennaro Contaldo

Raviolo with mushrooms and artichoke salad

Antonio Carluccio

Antonio's open raviolo with creamy mushroom and deliciously tender young artichoke is a modern pasta dish found in very good restaurants in Italy, where the filling can vary from fish and meat to vegetables or, in this case, mushrooms. Makes an impressive starter or light main.

For the raviolo, heat the butter in a pan, add the garlic and fry gently until softened but not browned. Add the mushrooms and stir-fry for about 5 minutes, then add the tomato purée, parsley and some salt and pepper. Pour in the wine, bring to the boil and let it bubble for a few minutes.

Cook the sheets of pasta in boiling salted water until al dente, then drain. A good tip is to add a couple of sheets of pasta at a time, so they don't stick together.

For the artichoke salad, trim the artichokes of all tough outer leaves and trim the stem to about 2cm long. Discard the spiky leaf tips, then slice the tender leaves and heart very thinly and put into a bowl of water with a splash of the lemon juice to prevent any discolouration until ready to serve.

Prepare the vinaigrette by whisking together the olive oil, remaining lemon juice and salt and pepper, to taste, in a small bowl.

To serve, carefully lay 4 sheets of pasta on 4 hot serving plates. Divide the mushroom mixture among them, reserving some of the sauce. Top the mushrooms with the remaining sheets of pasta and brush the top with the remaining sauce. Sprinkle with grated Parmesan, if you like.

Drain the artichokes and arrange them on the serving plates. Sprinkle with the Parmesan shavings, pour the vinaigrette over the artichokes, top with a little rocket and serve immediately.

Tip: This salad is best made with very fresh, small artichokes, picked before the choke has had a chance to form. The choke is the inedible hairy part at the centre of older artichokes. If you are using slightly larger artichokes, scrape out the choke, but take care to remove only the furry fibre because the meaty base of the artichoke underneath (the heart) is the tastiest bit.

Serves 4

60g butter
1 garlic clove, finely chopped
600g mixed wild mushrooms, cleaned and the larger ones cut in half
1 tbsp tomato purée
1 tbsp chopped flat-leaf parsley
125ml white wine
8 sheets fresh egg pasta (page 223), 15cm square
50g Parmesan, finely grated (optional)
sea salt and freshly ground black pepper

for the artichoke salad

8 young, tender globe artichokes
¼ lemon, juiced
6 tbsp extra virgin olive oil
sea salt and freshly ground black pepper

to serve

85g Parmesan (or a similar vegetarian hard cheese), shaved very thinly
handful of rocket

Tagliatelle with asparagus, lemon and pangritata

James Martin

Make the most of English asparagus with James's quick-and-easy pasta dish. Pangritata, also known as 'poor man's Parmesan', is breadcrumbs fried or toasted with garlic oil and herbs. It is a great way of adding flavour and crunch to your food, at very little expense.

First make the pangritata. Put the olive oil into a hot frying pan. Add the lemon zest, garlic, thyme, parsley, chilli and breadcrumbs and stir for a couple of minutes until the breadcrumbs are beautifully crisp and golden.

Cook the tagliatelle in salted boiling water until al dente.

While it is cooking, preheat a griddle pan and drizzle the olive oil over the asparagus. Add the asparagus and, once marked with bars from the griddle pan, add the butter, a little of the pasta water and lemon juice. Season with salt and pepper to taste.

To serve, remove the asparagus from the pan, cut into pieces and return to the pan. Add the asparagus and juices to the pasta and toss until all the pasta is coated. Add a couple of tablespoons of the pangritata and toss together.

Tip: Pangritata can be kept in the fridge for several days. Make a big batch of it and use it to jazz up seasonal greens, salads, fish or any simple pasta dish. You can substitute the thyme for rosemary or sage or other hardy, aromatic herbs.

Serves 6

for the pangritata
2 tbsp olive oil
1 lemon, zest and juice (reserve the juice for the tagliatelle)
1 garlic clove, finely chopped
2 tsp finely chopped thyme leaves
2 tbsp finely chopped flat-leaf parsley
1 red chilli, de-seeded, finely chopped
150g fresh breadcrumbs (any kind is fine)

for the tagliatelle and asparagus
500g fresh egg tagliatelle (to make your own, see page 223)
2 tbsp olive oil
1 bunch of asparagus, trimmed
50g butter
sea salt and freshly ground black pepper

Scotch egg with black pudding and pickled onion salad

Paul Ainsworth

Paul's gourmet Scotch egg is quite unusual and sure to delight foodies. As Paul says: 'I've always had smoked haddock on the menu in some way, as it is such an incredible ingredient. This version has got to be my favourite. There are so many textures to it, from the crispy, crunchy outside to the flavoursome fish, then the runny egg inside, which surprises people.' The challenge here is to make sure the yolk is runny in the centre, so follow the cooking times precisely.

To make the pickle, place the sugar, white wine vinegar and 25ml olive oil in a pan, pour in 300ml water and add salt, to taste. Bring to a simmer. Place the shallot rings in a bowl and pour the liquid over. Set aside to cool completely, then transfer to an airtight jar and leave to pickle for at least 24 hours.

Bring the eggs to room temperature before cooking or, if you're using the eggs straight from the fridge, add a small pinch of salt to the cooking water to help prevent cracking. Put the eggs into a pan in which they fit in a single layer. Add enough cold water to cover the eggs by 3cm and cover with a lid, then place the pan over a high heat. Once the water comes to a boil, remove the pan from the heat and allow to stand for 3 minutes, then transfer to a bowl of iced water until ready to use.

For the smoked haddock Scotch egg, preheat the oven to 180°C/350°F/Gas 4. Rub the potatoes in olive oil and rock salt and prick them half a dozen times all over. Wrap them in foil and bake in the oven for about an hour, or until soft. Leave to cool, then scoop out the potato and mash thoroughly. Cover with cling film and keep warm.

Put the haddock, spring onions and chives into a bowl. Mix in enough mashed potato to bind (you may not need all the potato). Add the sweet chilli sauce and lemon juice and season to taste with salt and pepper. Take a quarter of the mix in your hand and push it flat to form a rough circle approximately 5mm thick. Place a cooked and very carefully peeled egg in the middle and wrap the mixture gently around the egg. Repeat with the remaining eggs. Dip the Scotch eggs in the egg whites and gently shake off any excess, then coat in breadcrumbs.

Serves 4

for the pickled onion
100g sugar
100g white wine vinegar
40ml olive oil
2 banana shallots, peeled, sliced thinly

for the smoked haddock Scotch egg
4 medium eggs (Paul favours bantam)
2 large baking potatoes
olive oil
rock salt
350g smoked haddock fillet, chopped into cubes
3 spring onions, finely chopped
5g chives, chopped
35g sweet chilli sauce
½ lemon, juiced
2 egg whites, lightly whisked
200g breadcrumbs (ideally Japanese panko)
vegetable oil, for deep-frying
sea salt and freshly ground black pepper

to serve
curry mayonnaise (page 216)

Meanwhile, heat a deep-fat fryer or pour oil into a deep, heavy-based pan to a depth of at least 7cm and bring up to 180°C (or until a cube of white bread, when dropped in, turns light golden-brown in about 1 minute). Place the Scotch eggs carefully into the oil and fry for 2 minutes, or until golden-brown and crisp, then transfer to a plate lined with kitchen paper to drain.

To prepare the salad, heat the remaining olive oil in a frying pan, add the black pudding and fry until crisp, then drain on kitchen paper. Put the leaves in a salad bowl, add the black pudding, pickled shallots and chives, dress with vinaigrette and season to taste.

Serve the Scotch eggs whole or cut in half with the black pudding and pickled onion salad and, if using, a good dollop of curry mayonnaise on the side.

for the salad
70g good-quality black
   pudding, diced
2 Little Gem lettuces, leaves
   separated
20g chives, snipped
vinaigrette dressing
   (page 214), to taste
sea salt

Kedgeree

Lawrence Keogh

Fusing Indian spices with the best of British, kedgeree was a staple breakfast in Queen Victoria's day. Lawrence's version – a heap of creamy curried rice punctuated by generous chunks of smoky haddock and topped with a runny-middled poached egg – is so rich, so buttery, you'll happily eat it for breakfast, lunch or supper. Serve with some fresh crusty bread or a green salad.

Wash the rice several times until the water becomes clear. Add the rice, 1 litre water and the turmeric to a pan and bring to the boil. When boiling, cover with a lid and remove from the heat. Set aside for 20 minutes, then spread the cooked rice over a tray to cool.

For the haddock, place the milk and 500ml water in a large pan. Stud each half of the onion with a clove and bay leaf, then add to the milk and bring to the boil. Place the haddock in a deep roasting tin and pour over the hot milk. Cover with cling film very quickly to seal in the steam and heat. Set aside for approximately 45 minutes.

Remove the cling film and transfer the haddock to a plate. Remove the fish skin and any bones and leave it chunky and as whole as possible.

For the sauce, in a large pan gently fry the onion, garlic and ginger in the sunflower oil until the onion is light golden-brown. Add the Madras paste and cook for 5 minutes, then add the chilli, star anise and bay leaf. Add 100ml water and simmer until the volume of liquid has reduced by half.

Add the double cream and simmer for 10 minutes, then transfer to a blender and pulse until smooth. Season to taste with salt and pepper.

To serve, transfer the sauce to a pan and bring to a simmer. Add the rice and gently reheat. Fold in three-quarters of the haddock and heat through.

Meanwhile, fill a large pan with boiling water, add the white wine vinegar and poach the eggs to your liking.

At the last minute, add the remaining haddock and chopped parsley and serve in warm bowls with a poached egg on top. Finish with a spoonful of melted butter, a sprinkle of coriander and a little salt and pepper.

Tip: It's important that you cool the rice before reheating so that you don't end up with a mushy mess. It is even quicker to use leftover rice: it keeps brilliantly in the freezer until ready to use.

Serves 4

for the haddock and rice

500g basmati rice
2 tsp turmeric
500ml milk
1 onion, peeled, halved
2 cloves
2 bay leaves
500g smoked haddock fillet, pin boned
1 tsp white wine vinegar
4 eggs, for poaching
2 tbsp chopped flat-leaf parsley
knob of butter, melted
1 punnet coriander cress or coriander leaves
sea salt

for the sauce

1 onion, finely chopped
1 garlic clove, peeled, crushed
2cm piece fresh ginger, peeled, chopped
100ml sunflower oil
60g Madras paste (page 218)
1 red chilli, chopped
1 star anise
1 bay leaf
400ml double cream
sea salt and freshly ground black pepper

Prawn laksa soup

Ching-He Huang

Ching's classic prawn laksa is a rich curry broth with Indian, Thai, Malaysian and Chinese influences. It makes a wonderfully warming meal with aromatic spices, coconutty rice noodles and a little heat. Once you have all the ingredients, the yellow curry paste is whizzed up in less than a minute, and the rest of the recipe is surprisingly quick to make. Laksa is delicious with seafood, such as prawns or crab, but the basic laksa recipe works well with chicken, pork, fried tofu, egg or whatever seasonal vegetables you fancy.

Put the ingredients for the laksa paste into a blender or food processor and process to a fine, smooth paste.

For the crispy prawn garnish, put 2 tablespoons of the laksa paste into a bowl and add 4 of the whole prawns. Cover and set aside in the fridge to marinate while you make the soup.

For the soup, heat 2 tablespoons of vegetable oil in a large wok and cook the remaining laksa paste for 1 minute until it deepens in colour. Stir in the coconut milk, stock, dried kaffir lime leaves, sugar and fish sauce and 300ml water. Bring the soup to the boil and simmer for 20 minutes until the flavour deepens.

A few minutes before the soup is ready, prepare the crispy prawn garnish. Take the 4 marinated prawns out of the curry marinade, season with a couple of pinches of sea salt and black pepper and sprinkle over the potato flour. Heat a small pan, add the remaining 2 tablespoons of vegetable oil and cook the prawns for 1½ minutes on each side until golden-brown, crisp and cooked through. Take off the heat, but leave them in the pan to keep warm.

To finish the soup, add the vermicelli rice noodles and stir while cooking for 2 minutes. Then add the remaining prawns and cook for 2 minutes. Season the soup with lime juice (or salt and chilli powder/flakes, if preferred), add the bean sprouts and spring onion. Remove the kaffir lime leaves, give it a final stir and then it is ready to serve.

Divide the noodles evenly among the bowls and ladle over the soup. Garnish with the fried prawns, coriander leaves and extra lime wedges.

Tip: You can buy potato flour, which is sometimes called potato starch, from Asian supermarkets or online. If you can't get any, substitute with rice flour or cornflour.

Serves 4

for the laksa paste
1 tsp ground coriander
1 tsp ground cumin
1 tsp turmeric
2 small onions, chopped
50ml coconut milk
2.5cm piece fresh ginger, peeled, roughly chopped
2 garlic cloves, crushed
2 lemongrass stalks, roughly chopped
2 hot red chillies, de-seeded, roughly chopped
1 tbsp fermented shrimp paste

for the prawn noodle soup and crispy prawn garnish
400g raw prawns, de-veined, with tails on
4 tbsp vegetable oil
350ml coconut milk
500ml chicken stock (page 214)
2 dried kaffir lime leaves
1 tbsp brown sugar
3–4 tbsp fish sauce
2 tbsp potato flour
100g dried vermicelli rice noodles
1 large lime, juiced or chilli powder or flakes, to taste (optional)
80g bean sprouts
1 large spring onion, sliced on a deep angle in 1cm pieces
handful of coriander leaves, to garnish
1 large lime, sliced into wedges, to garnish
sea salt and freshly ground black pepper

Menu: Go Latino!

Latin American food is the latest hot culinary trend, delivering a strong kick of flavour, exotic, healthy ingredients and a unique blend of indigenous and global cooking traditions. These simple recipes, from the UK's hottest Peruvian and Mexican chefs, make a fun and interesting dinner for friends. Finish off with a batch of little fudge biscuits and serve with a jug of ice-cold beer.

Starter

Palm heart salad by Martin Morales (page 27)

_____

Main

Braised and pulled beef tacos by Fernando Stovell (page 28)

_____

Dessert

Little fudge biscuits by Martin Morales (page 180)

_____

Palm heart salad

Martin Morales

The flavours of Peruvian food are unique, but you shouldn't struggle to find the ingredients for this salad. It is best made using tinned palm hearts, which are increasingly available in the UK (and easy to order online). If you can't get them, substitute with Peru's most famous crop – the potato – to make a very good potato salad.

Put the palm hearts, olives, chilli and feta in a large bowl and mix together.

Mix the dressing ingredients together in a bowl or jug and pour over the salad ingredients. Toss gently. Check for seasoning and add salt and pepper if necessary.

Divide the spinach among the serving plates and top with the dressed salad. Sprinkle with alfalfa sprouts to serve.

Serves 4–6

300g tinned palm hearts (or waxy potatoes), drained and cut into 5mm slices
100g pitted kalamata olives, chopped
1 amarillo or jalapeño chilli, finely diced
150g feta, crumbled
70g baby leaf spinach
3 tbsp alfalfa sprouts

for the dressing
4 tbsp extra virgin olive oil
1 lime, juiced
sea salt and freshly ground black pepper

Braised and pulled beef tacos

Fernando Stovell

Any good butcher will sell brisket. It's a fantastic, cheap cut of meat from the breast or lower chest, full of fat and connective tissues, which break down over long, slow cooking to produce flavoursome, fall-apart goodness. Fernando's tacos make a relaxed, hands-on Mexican feast. Prepare the meat a day or so in advance. Then, when Martin's salad is eaten, put a basket of tortillas on the table (with a cloth inside to keep them warm), add bowls of the beef salad, sliced lettuce and avocado, and let everyone help themselves!

Preheat the oven to 150°C/300°F/Gas 2.

Season the beef brisket with salt and freshly ground black pepper. Heat the oil in a large frying pan over a medium heat. Add the brisket and fry for 3–4 minutes, turning regularly, or until browned on all sides. Transfer the beef to a large casserole dish and add the onion, garlic and stock. If necessary, top up the dish with enough water to cover the beef. Cover the dish with a lid and cook in the oven for 2½–3 hours, then remove from the oven and leave to rest for 20 minutes before shredding the meat with two forks or your hands (remove any sinew and gristle as you shred the meat).

For the salsa, preheat the grill to its highest setting. Place the tomatoes, the onion wedge and the whole green chillies under the grill and leave for 3–4 minutes, or until the vegetables are slightly blackened (remove the onion and chillies before the tomatoes, as they will blacken first). Transfer the blackened vegetables to a pestle and mortar (or a food processor) and blend until smooth. Season, to taste, with salt. Sprinkle over the chopped onion, then set aside for at least 20 minutes.

Meanwhile, mix all the salad ingredients except the coriander together. Add the beef to the bowl and stir until well combined, then add the coriander and season, to taste, with salt and freshly ground black pepper.

When you are ready to serve, put the beef salad, salsa, lettuce and avocado slices in little bowls for people to build their own tacos.

Tip: If you're not going to use all the leftover brisket within 2 or 3 days, simply portion it up and freeze for future meals. Defrost in the fridge for 24 hours before cooking.

Serves 6

for the beef
750g boneless beef brisket
   or flank
2 tbsp sunflower oil
1 small onion, roughly
   chopped
2 garlic cloves, peeled
1 litre beef stock
sea salt and freshly ground
   black pepper

for the salsa
3 tomatoes
½ small onion, peeled,
   halved, one half left as
   a wedge, one half finely
   chopped
2 small green chillies
sea salt

for the salad
1 medium onion, finely sliced
2 small tomatoes, seeds
   removed, finely chopped
6 tbsp grapeseed oil (or extra
   virgin olive oil)
3 tbsp malt vinegar
1 jalapeño or bird's-eye chilli,
   de-seeded, finely chopped
10 pitted green olives, sliced
1 tsp chopped fresh oregano
3 tbsp chopped coriander
   leaves

to serve
12 ready-made taco shells
½ iceberg lettuce, core
   removed, finely sliced
1 ripe avocado, peeled,
   stone removed, sliced
   lengthways

Whole sea bream with lemon and chilli

Angela Hartnett

Served with a spinach, new potato and parsley salad, Angela's Mediterranean classic is simple, tasty and very quick to prepare. Once cooked, the fillets of sea bream will easily pull away from the bones, making it easy to serve – and eat!

Preheat the oven to 200°C/400°F/Gas 6.

For the baked sea bream, stuff the cavity of the fish with the garlic, red chilli, onion (or leek), parsley and half of the sliced lemons. Put the fish on a baking tray and place the remaining lemon slices and thyme leaves on top. Pour over the white wine, drizzle with olive oil and cover with foil.

Bake for 10–15 minutes, or until the fish is cooked through.

For the spinach, new potato and parsley salad, heat a pan of boiling water and cook the potatoes for 10–15 minutes. Drain and place into a large serving bowl.

Add the baby spinach and parsley. Stir and season to taste with salt and pepper.

In a small bowl, add the olive oil, white wine vinegar and Dijon mustard and whisk to combine. Pour the dressing over the salad just before serving.

To serve, place the whole sea bream on a serving dish and serve the salad alongside.

Tip: This method of cooking, with foil covering the fish, essentially steams it, making the flavours very intense. It is a great way of ensuring your fish is tender and is an easy and very healthy way of cooking any whole fish. Try the same method with trout or sea bass.

Serves 4

for the sea bream
4 whole sea bream, gutted
   and cleaned
4 garlic cloves, peeled,
   roughly chopped
2 red chillies, finely sliced
2 small onions, thickly sliced
   or 2 leeks, sliced
4 tbsp chopped flat-leaf
   parsley
2 lemons, sliced
2 tbsp chopped thyme leaves
200ml white wine
100ml olive oil

for the salad
400g new potatoes
100g baby spinach
4 tbsp roughly chopped
   flat-leaf parsley
6 tbsp olive oil
2 tbsp white wine vinegar
2 tsp Dijon mustard
sea salt and freshly ground
   black pepper

Roasted monkfish with Iberico ham, peas, broad beans, morels and English asparagus

Clare Smyth

Monkfish is quite a meaty fish and it can carry other strong flavours easily, so Clare makes this a dish to savour with slices of salty Iberico ham, earthy morels and the bright spring flavours of English asparagus, broad beans and peas. The combination is stunning!

For the parsley butter, heat the olive oil in a pan and fry the shallot, mushrooms and garlic until they are softened. Set aside to cool.

Mix the shallot and mushroom mixture in a bowl with the butter and chopped parsley. Set aside.

For the monkfish, preheat the oven to 230°C/450°F/Gas 8 and clean the morels thoroughly.

Heat a dash of olive oil in a saucepan and fry the shallots and morels for 2–4 minutes. Add the white wine and chicken or fish stock and cook for about 6–8 minutes, or until the volume of liquid has significantly reduced. Add the broad beans and then the peas and stir through a little of the parsley butter.

Place the asparagus in a pan with a little olive oil, salt and a splash of stock and put a lid on. Cook for 2–4 minutes – it will steam in its own juices.

Heat another dash of olive oil in an ovenproof pan and cook the monkfish for 2 minutes on each side, or until nicely browned all over. Transfer to the oven to finish cooking for 4 minutes. Once out of the oven, place a slice of ham on top of each portion of fish so that it starts to melt while resting. Leave to rest for at least 4 minutes.

To serve, spoon the buttery peas, broad beans and morels onto each plate, then the asparagus and morels. Place the monkfish on top. Save the juices from the morels and the asparagus pans. Add another splash of olive oil and lemon juice to the combined pan juices and use this as a sauce. Serve any remaining parsley butter on the side.

Serves 4

for the parsley butter
splash olive oil
½ shallot, finely chopped
50g button mushrooms, finely chopped
1 garlic clove, finely chopped
80g butter, cut into cubes, at room temperature
10g chopped flat-leaf parsley

for the monkfish
100g morel mushrooms, cleaned
olive oil
2 shallots, finely chopped
100ml white wine
250ml chicken or fish stock (page 214), plus a splash of stock to cook the asparagus
100g podded broad beans
100g peas
12 spears asparagus, tough ends removed
4 fillets monkfish, about 130–150g each
50g Iberico ham, thinly sliced
1 lemon, juiced
sea salt

Poussin scented with ginger and lemongrass

Michel Roux

Michel's Asian-inspired dish makes a simple mid-week supper, with a beautifully elegant presentation and a lovely balance of flavours.

Put 1.5 litres of water into a steamer pan, salt very lightly, cover and bring to the boil. Meanwhile, mix the ginger with the lemongrass and place inside the poussins (they don't need trussing). Put them in the top of the steamer, cover and steam for 15–20 minutes.

Scatter over the broccoli florets and cook for another 2 minutes. Transfer the broccoli to a bowl, cover with cling film and keep warm.

Cut off the legs and breasts from the poussins. Wrap the breasts in foil and leave to rest in a warm place. Reserve the legs.

Break up the carcasses and put them in the cooking water in the base of the steamer, together with the ginger and lemongrass mixture (from inside the poussins). Simmer for 5 minutes, add the blended cornflour and cook, stirring, for 1 minute, then strain through a fine sieve into a saucepan. Adjust the seasoning if necessary. Keep the sauce warm.

Heat the grapeseed oil in a frying pan. Add the poussin legs, skin-side down, and fry over a medium heat until the skin is slightly crunchy and a beautiful light golden-brown. Repeat with the chicken breasts.

Heat a deep-fat fryer or pour oil into a deep, heavy-based pan to a depth of at least 7cm and bring up to 160°C. Make sure the rocket (or parsley) is completely dry. Put it into the hot oil and deep-fry until very crisp, stirring with a slotted spoon, then drain on kitchen paper. If the rocket isn't as crisp as it should be, reheat the oil and fry it for another 2–3 minutes. Drain on kitchen paper and salt lightly.

To serve, pile the hot rice on a plate and arrange the poussin breasts and legs on top. Scatter on little heaps of broccoli and rocket and serve at once, handing the sauce round separately.

Tip: If there is any chicken or rice left over, shred the chicken, fold it into the rice and serve with soy sauce and wasabi on the side. It is so fresh and light; a dish in itself.

Serves 4

20g fresh ginger, peeled, thinly sliced
2 lemongrass stalks, cut lengthways into strips
2 poussins (350g each), wishbones removed
200g tenderstem broccoli
1 tbsp cornflour, mixed with 2 tbsp cold water
2 tbsp grapeseed oil (or extra virgin olive oil)
vegetable oil, for frying
110g rocket leaves or flat-leaf parsley
sea salt and freshly ground black pepper

to serve

200g Thai long-grain rice, steamed

Spring

Roast duck breast, wild garlic gnocchi, five spice, oranges and caramel

James Tanner

James's reworking of a French classic, 'duck à l'orange', uses the subtle flavour of wild garlic to transform a simple, homemade gnocchi and bitter-sweet citrus sauce. Wild garlic (ramsons) is the ultimate foraging ingredient: it's healthy and grows abundantly at this time of year – look out for clumps of bright green, pointy leaves and that distinctive garlicky smell (or buy bunches at farmers' markets). The star-shaped white garlic flowers are edible too, and make a pretty garnish, but the plant is at its best before too many flowers appear.

Preheat the oven to 180°C/350°F/Gas 4.

Scrub the potatoes, dry them well and prick all over, then arrange on a baking tray and bake for an hour until the flesh is fluffy and completely cooked through.

Meanwhile, heat a saucepan and add the wild garlic with a knob of butter and fry gently, while stirring, for around 30 seconds until the leaves are wilted. Season with salt and freshly ground black pepper, then remove from the heat and tip out onto kitchen paper to soak up any excess liquid. When cool enough, roughly chop.

Remove the cooked potatoes from the oven and as soon as they're cool enough to handle, cut in half, scoop out the flesh and discard the skins. Pass the potato flesh through a ricer, or sieve, into a large bowl. Add the egg yolk and flour, a little at a time, and mix with the potatoes and cooked wild garlic until they come together into a soft, light dough.

Dust a work surface with a little flour and divide the dough into six pieces. Use your hands to roll each piece into long (about 45cm) sausage shapes. Lay the sausages side by side, cut them into 2cm pieces with a blunt table knife and place on a bed of semolina on a tray. Pop in the fridge for about 10 minutes to set.

Meanwhile, for the duck, preheat the oven to 200°C/400°F/Gas 6.

Heat a medium non-stick pan, prick the skin and season the duck breasts all over. Cook, skin-side down, with no oil for 4 minutes over a medium heat, then turn, rolling the breast in the rendered fat to seal all over. Spoon out the excess fat (there'll be lots of it) to save for frying potatoes, then return the duck breasts to the pan, skin-side down again, and transfer the pan to the oven. Roast for 6–8 minutes.

Serves 2–4

for the wild garlic gnocchi
500g King Edward potatoes, about 3 large potatoes (Maris Piper or Desiree will also work)
2 large handfuls wild garlic, washed and picked (reserve any flowers for the garnish)
50g butter
1 egg yolk
200–250g plain flour
30g semolina
sea salt and freshly ground black pepper

for the duck
2 duck breasts, sinew and small fillet removed
1 tbsp blossom honey
1 tsp five spice

Remove the duck breasts from the oven and again drain off any excess fat. With the pan back on the hob, mix the honey and five spice together and coat the duck breasts in the hot pan.

Remove from the heat, transfer onto a plate and set aside to rest.

Meanwhile, for the sauce, put the orange and lime zest in a hot pan and sprinkle over the sugar. Keep the heat high, stirring occasionally, until the sugar turns to a golden caramel. Then add the citrus juice and continue to cook, so the caramel dissolves, and the liquid is reduced by half. Add the wine and stock, then simmer until the sauce is thick enough to coat the back of a spoon. Strain the sauce through a sieve, discard the zest, and set the sauce aside until needed.

When you are ready to eat, cook the gnocchi in a pan of salted simmering water for about 2–3 minutes, or until they float to the top, then use a slotted spoon to lift them out of the pan. Warm the citrus sauce and drop in the broad beans and orange segments and whisk in a knob of butter.

In a non-stick frying pan, melt a knob of butter, add the gnocchi, and toss over a high heat for 3 minutes, until golden. Season with sea salt and plenty of freshly ground black pepper.

To serve, carve the duck into thick slices and arrange on plates with the gnocchi. Spoon and drizzle the sauce over and around. Finally, finish with a scatter of picked watercress leaves, the reserved wild garlic flowers (if you have any) and a drizzle of extra virgin olive oil.

for the citrus sauce
1 orange, half zested and
  juiced, other half cut into
  segments
1 lime, half zested, whole
  juiced
1 tbsp caster sugar
75ml red wine (Merlot is
  good)
150ml strong beef stock
110g double-podded broad
  beans
knob of butter

to serve
1 small bunch watercress,
  leaves picked
drizzle extra virgin olive oil

Tandoori chicken with lentil salad

Atul Kochhar

This dish would take minutes to bake in a traditional tandoor (a basic clay oven, with a fire at the bottom), but Atul shows how to cook the meat fast and seal in the flavour using a domestic oven or grill the chicken on a hot barbecue to add a lovely, smoky element to the dish. Don't expect your marinade to be a pillar-box red – in India this would come from an abundance of Kashmiri chillies and these are not widely available here – but if you prefer a bit of colour, Atul suggests adding a little saffron water or orange food dye to the mix.

Make deep incisions into the chicken breasts, thighs and drumsticks. Whisk the yoghurt in a large bowl, add the remaining marinade ingredients and mix until well combined. Rub the marinade over the chicken until it is completely coated, then chill in the fridge for 3–4 hours.

Preheat the oven to 200°C/400°F/Gas 6.

Place the chicken on a rack above a roasting tray and cook in the oven for 15–20 minutes (or on a barbecue for about 12–15 minutes) until cooked.

Preheat the grill to high. Remove the chicken from the oven and rest for 2–3 minutes. Baste thoroughly with butter and roast under the grill for 3–4 minutes, or until the juices run clear when the chicken is pierced with a skewer and it is completely cooked through.

Just before serving, mix all the salad ingredients together in a big bowl. Whisk the dressing ingredients together until well combined and pour it over the salad.

Dust the chicken with chat masala, and add a squeeze of lime from the wedges and serve with the lentil salad and mint chutney on the side.

Tip: Double the amount of marinade and freeze the excess for a later date – it's great with fish, lamb or pork.

Serves 4–6

for the chicken
2 whole chickens, skinned, jointed (ask your butcher to do this)
200g plain yoghurt
2 tsp ginger and garlic paste (garlic, ginger and vegetable oil, blended to a paste)
½ tsp chilli powder
1 tsp ground coriander
¼ tsp ground cinnamon
½ tsp garam masala
2 tsp lemon juice
½ tsp mango powder
½ tsp ground fenugreek leaves
1 tbsp gram flour
1 tsp saffron water or ¼ tsp edible orange colour (optional)
1 tsp vegetable oil
pinch sea salt
50g melted butter, for basting

for the lentil salad
200g chickpeas, sprouted or cooked
110g green lentils, sprouted or cooked
small bunch watercress
small bunch (baby red) chard leaves or baby spinach
1 tomato, chopped
1 red onion, chopped
1 cucumber, chopped
1 tbsp chopped coriander leaves
½ tsp grated fresh ginger

for the dressing
3 tbsp vegetable oil
1 tsp lime juice
pinch salt
pinch sugar
1 green chilli, chopped
    (optional)
½ tsp cumin seeds, toasted,
    ground
1 tsp chat masala (available
    from specialist Asian
    stores)

to serve
1 tbsp chat masala
2 limes, sliced into wedges
mint chutney (to make your
    own, see page 218)

Spring

Rosemary and garlic salt baked lamb shank with pickled cabbage salad and sweet mustard mayonnaise

Tom Kerridge

This is a great dish – delicious, doable and ideal for a colder spring day. The lamb shank is a meaty cut from the lower end of the leg. It's big on flavour and becomes meltingly tender when baked long and slow in Tom's ingenious salt pastry crust. If you're able to find nasturtium leaves they make a very pretty garnish for this dish.

First, blitz the rosemary and salt together in a food processor until mixed. In a food mixer fitted with the dough hook, bring together the flour and rosemary salt, then add the egg whites. Slowly add up to 300ml water – you may not need it all. Once it comes together in a dough, knead it using the machine for about 5 minutes. Remove the dough from the mixer, wrap in cling film and allow to rest for 2 hours.

Preheat the oven to 150°C/300°F/Gas 2. Roll out the salt dough into a rectangle about 1cm thick. Cut into 4 equal rectangles.

Blend the garlic cloves to a paste with around 50ml water. Brush all over the lamb shanks. Wrap each lamb shank in a piece of dough with the bone sticking out of the top. Place in a roasting tray and bake in the preheated oven for 4½ hours. Remove and rest for 30 minutes.

Meanwhile, for the pickling liquor, place all the ingredients except the cabbage into a saucepan and bring to the boil. Remove from the heat and infuse for 30 minutes. Strain the liquor through a sieve into a bowl and leave to cool. Place the raw cut-up cabbage into the pickle mix and leave for at least an hour.

For the salad, mix all the onions together with the chilli, sprinkle with the sea salt and leave for 20 minutes to break down. Drain the pickled cabbage and mix with the onion salad. Sprinkle with the chopped chives and drizzle with rapeseed oil.

For the mayonnaise, place all the ingredients except the oil into a food processor and blend to a fine purée. Gradually add the vegetable oil, while the food processor is running, until the mayonnaise has thickened. Season with a little salt.

To serve, break open the crust around the lamb and serve each lamb shank with the pickled cabbage salad and mustard mayonnaise.

Serves 4

for the lamb
75g rosemary, leaves picked
300g salt
1kg plain flour
9 egg whites
1 head garlic, separated into
    cloves, peeled
4 lamb shanks, fully trimmed

for the pickled cabbage
500ml white wine vinegar
½ cinnamon stick
4 star anise
1 tsp fennel seeds
1 tbsp coriander seeds
300g caster sugar
1 tsp white peppercorns
1 tsp Sichuan pepper
1 cabbage, cut into chunks

for the salad
1 onion, thinly sliced
2 bunches spring onions,
    sliced
1 red onion, thinly sliced
1 green chilli, sliced
1–2 tbsp sea salt
1 bunch chives, chopped
200ml rapeseed oil

for the sweet mustard mayo
1 egg yolk
2 tbsp English mustard
2 tsp white wine vinegar
2 tsp caster sugar
1 tsp lemon juice
325ml vegetable oil
sea salt

Spring

Short rib of beef with mussels, parsley and garlic

Glynn Purnell

Slow roasted in red wine and paired with mussels cooked in a luscious wild garlic sauce, these short ribs taste amazing. The cut, otherwise known as 'Jacob's Ladder' or 'oven-buster' (because the meat swells up when you cook it on the bone) is the small rack of ribs from the forequarter flank, marbled with fat and richly flavoured. Your butcher may need a couple of days to order this in, so plan ahead. You could also brine and cook the ribs in advance (they taste even better the next day).

For the short ribs, preheat the oven to 190°C/375°F/Gas 5.

Heat a large ovenproof frying pan and add the butter. When it is melted and foaming, add the short ribs and seal the beef until browned all over. Add the vegetables, herbs and peppercorns. Pour in the wine and stock and cover with foil. Place in the oven for 3 hours, or until the meat is very tender.

When the short ribs are cooked, remove from the oven and set aside to rest. Pass the cooking juices through a fine sieve and return to the pan. Cook over a medium-high heat until the volume of liquid has reduced to a thick glaze.

Meanwhile, discard any mussels with broken shells or open shells that do not close when given a sharp tap. Heat a large saucepan and melt the butter, then add the shallots, garlic and parsley stalks. Add the mussels and cider. Place a lid on the pan and cook the mussels for 3–4 minutes, or until the shells are open (discard any unopened shells). Drain the mussels, reserving the cooking liquor. Remove half the mussels from their shells.

Place the reserved mussel juices in a frying pan and bring to a simmer. Whisk in half the garlic and parsley butter and cook until thickened. Add the mussels (both in and out of the shells) and remove from the heat.

To serve, shred the beef and divide among serving plates. Pour over the glaze. Warm the mussels in the remaining garlic and parsley butter and serve over the top of the beef. Garnish with baby watercress or some sprigs of parsley.

Tip: Immersing meat in brine for a short period of time is a great way of ensuring the seasoning is evenly distributed throughout. After just a few hours the salt will be nicely permeated through the meat and it will not require further seasoning.

Serves 4

for the short ribs
2 tbsp butter
4 bone-in beef short ribs (about 2.5kg), cut in 2 (ask your butcher to do this), soaked in brine for 3 hours (page 213)
1 carrot, peeled, roughly chopped
1 onion, roughly chopped
2 sticks celery, roughly chopped
1 garlic clove, sliced
3 thyme sprigs
2 bay leaves
4 black peppercorns
250ml red wine
250ml beef stock

for the mussels
1.5kg mussels, scrubbed and debearded
25g butter
2 shallots, finely chopped
1 garlic clove, sliced
2 tbsp chopped parsley stalks
200ml dry cider
4 tbsp garlic and parsley butter (see page 219)

for the garnish
handful baby watercress or parsley sprigs (optional)

Menu: Easter

Easter is the best of times for foodies, coinciding with the arrival of warmer weather and beautiful spring ingredients. Francesco combines some of Italy's finest produce for his stunning salad, whilst Gennaro keeps it simple with slow-cooked shoulder of lamb and peas. Finish with a celebratory orange and almond cake, shop-bought panettone or an Easter egg hunt in the garden, if the sun is out.

Starter

Artichoke salad by Francesco Mazzei (page 47)

Main

Easter lamb with peas by Gennaro Contaldo (page 48)

Dessert

Orange and almond cake by James Martin (page 186)

Artichoke salad

Francesco Mazzei

At this time of year, the most delicious artichokes come from Italy. Francesco favours the fat, round variety, known as mammole, which grow in and around Rome. Or you could wait for British-grown globe artichokes (such as Green Globe) – the season starts in May.

Remove the tough leaves from each artichoke and cut off the stalk. Throw away the first round leaves as they are too bitter. Reserve the remainder of the tough outer leaves, the stem and the very centre part of the artichoke (the choke) for the stock. Separate the tender leaves from the rest and rub the tender leaves from each artichoke with a cut lemon so they don't discolour, then place in a bowl of water for later (they will be eaten raw).

In a medium-sized pan, gently fry the garlic and shallots in a little olive oil until golden-brown. Add the anchovies, white wine and reserved tough artichoke leaves and stem. Cook until the wine has evaporated completely.

Add a generous pinch of sea salt and freshly ground black pepper, then the sugar, mint, breadcrumbs, 20g of the grated Parmesan and the vegetable stock. Simmer for approximately 30 minutes. Set aside to cool.

In the meantime, zest and juice the lemons, then mix the avocado with the chopped chillies, a little lemon juice and the lemon zest. Season to taste with salt and freshly ground black pepper.

Chop the raw artichoke leaves into a fine julienne. Toss in some lemon juice and salt. Mix with the avocado and set aside.

Make a dressing by passing the artichoke cooking liquor through a fine sieve (try to get about 4 tablespoons of cooking liquor). Mix with the olive oil and a squeeze of lemon juice.

To serve, spoon the avocado and artichoke mixture into a 10cm metal chefs' ring sitting in the middle of each serving plate. Press down gently to compact. Using a palette knife, smooth the top, then carefully remove the metal ring. Arrange the celery cress on top with shavings of Parmesan. Drizzle the dressing around the plate and finish with the remaining grated Parmesan.

Tip: Francesco's elegant presentation will delight the eye, but if you don't have the right assembly tools, or a sprinkling of cress, a more rustic presentation will still delight the palate.

Serves 4–6

12 mammole (or other globe) artichokes
6 unwaxed lemons, 1 cut in half
1 head garlic, peeled, roughly chopped
450g shallots, roughly chopped
24 anchovy fillets
750ml white wine
30g sugar
small bunch mint, leaves only
60g white breadcrumbs
75g Parmesan (or a similar vegetarian hard cheese), grated
4½ litres vegetable stock, cooled
6 large avocados, peeled, stone removed and chopped
6 red chillies, finely chopped
12 tbsp extra virgin olive oil
sea salt and freshly ground black pepper

to serve

3 tbsp celery cress (optional)
25g Parmesan shavings

Easter lamb with peas

Gennaro Contaldo

Gennaro says, 'It is very traditional to eat the new season's lamb with fresh peas at Easter in Italy, and a dish such as this is not uncommon for lunch on Easter Sunday, when the whole family will gather together to celebrate one of the most important religious feasts of the year.'

Season the lamb chunks with salt and pepper and set aside. Heat the olive oil in a large pan and sweat the onion, carrot and celery until soft. Add the garlic, anchovies, thyme and chilli and continue to cook, stirring, until the anchovies have almost dissolved into the oil. Add the lamb chunks and seal well all over. Stir in the wine and allow to reduce down by half, then add the vinegar.

Reduce the heat to low, cover and simmer gently for 20 minutes. Add the peas, potatoes and tomatoes, cover again and continue to cook for about an hour, until the sauce has reduced by half. Remove from the heat and serve with lots of good toasted bread.

Tip: The secret to success with this recipe is in leaving the lamb to cook over a very low heat. In this way, the lamb and the rest of the ingredients will cook through well, and all the juices will ooze out to create a lovely sauce.

Serves 6

1kg boned lamb shoulder,
    cut into large chunks
10 tbsp extra virgin olive oil
2 onions, roughly chopped
1 large carrot, sliced
1 stick celery, roughly
    chopped
5 garlic cloves, peeled,
    crushed
20g anchovy fillets
handful thyme sprigs
1 red chilli, sliced
250ml white wine
25ml white wine vinegar
250g fresh or frozen peas
400g potatoes, skins left on,
    cut into quarters
200g cherry tomatoes,
    halved
sea salt and freshly ground
    black pepper

When I think of summer, I think of tomatoes, Italy, salads, basil, beans...
I could go on and on.

Sitting outside and eating the season's produce al fresco is really one of life's
pleasures, and there's nothing better than cooking outside and then eating with a
group of friends whilst you watch the sun go down.

For me, one of the main draws of summer and its ingredients is the fruit. Not just
English strawberries, but beautiful peaches and nectarines, apricots and Scottish
raspberries too. It's a classic combination, but strawberries are fantastic with a
dollop of fresh cream – and for gatherings I like to make mini pavlovas with them.
The balance of crunchy, chewy meringue, sweet summer fruit and luxurious cream
is stunning.

A fresh peach can be just perfect on its own. I still think of one summer years ago
when I went to Italy and must have eaten at least five peaches a day. My aunt kept
count and pointed it out to me. There's really nothing like the juice and sweetness
of peaches when they're ripe and I've ruined numerous shirts and T-shirts with
juice stains.

Summer is also the time you start to plot for the winter months ahead. Towards
the end of the season, when you may be left with a glut of produce about to turn
overripe, is the time to start pickling vegetables and making jam with the last
summer fruits. I find the process exciting as just when I may have had my fill of a
particular ingredient, preserving opens up new possibilities for delicious dishes.
Lemons, for example, are delicious squeezed fresh over salad leaves and fish
dishes, or in a sorbet; but if you pack them with salt to preserve them, they take on
an incredibly complex, sour flavour that can enhance Middle-Eastern-style tagines
or warm salads.

We are blessed in this country with having amazing shellfish: lobster, crabs and
langoustines can epitomise the simplicity of summer, as there's nothing easier
than serving a fresh crab with a pot of homemade mayonnaise. It's so basic, but
nothing tastes better.

My favourite types of meals, and those I like to cook, are those in which a few good
ingredients are treated simply so that their flavours shine through. Suffice to say,
I love the summer for this reason, when ingredients taste so good you hardly need
to cook.

Angela Hartnett

Stuffed courgette flowers

Katie Caldesi

Courgette flowers are one of the easiest – and quickest – crops to grow in a plant pot or your garden. The male flowers have long, spiky stalks, which make for easier dipping into the hot batter and hot oil. Cut the courgettes almost in half, but not right through from the base to the tip, to allow the heat of the oil to penetrate.

To prepare the flowers, pinch out the bitter stamens with your fingertips, trying not to break the flower, and check for any bugs inside.

To make the batter, whisk the egg and 2 tablespoons of the milk in a large bowl for 1 minute. Whisk in the flour, a little at a time, then whisk in the beer (or sparkling water), salt, sugar and the remaining milk. If any lumps remain, sieve the mixture before dipping in the flowers.

Heat the oil to 180°C in a deep-fat fryer or high-sided frying pan (or until a cube of white bread, when dropped in, turns light golden brown in about 1 minute).

Meanwhile, mix the ricotta, Parmesan, Parma ham, basil, nutmeg and lemon zest in a bowl until combined. Finely chop the mozzarella and add half to the mixture. Season to taste with salt and freshly ground black pepper.

Use a piping bag or teaspoon to fill half the flowers with the stuffing, then twist the flowers at the top to close them.

Stuff the remaining mozzarella inside the remaining courgette flowers and place an anchovy inside each flower. Twist the ends closed.

Stir the batter (do this before each dip to keep the batter at the right consistency). Dip a couple of flowers into the batter and fry for about 5 minutes, until golden brown. Remove with tongs, drain on kitchen paper and keep warm. Continue dipping and frying in batches until you have finished.

Serve with a dusting of sea salt and either a tomato sauce or a light tomato salad, with lemon wedges to squeeze.

Tip: You can also serve the courgette flowers with a light salad of grated vegetables and a drizzle of bright green basil oil.

Serves 4

8 courgette flowers
1 egg
100ml whole milk
110g plain flour
60ml beer or sparkling water
¼ tsp sea salt
¼ tsp caster sugar
sunflower or olive oil, for
    deep-frying

for the stuffing
100g ricotta
30g Parmesan, grated
25g Parma ham, finely
    chopped
handful basil leaves, torn
pinch grated nutmeg
½ lemon, zest only
200g mozzarella
4 anchovy fillets
sea salt and freshly ground
    black pepper

to serve
quick tomato sauce (page
    217) or ripe tomatoes,
    diced
1 lemon, cut into wedges
sea salt

Summer

Grilled goat's cheese and courgette salad

James Martin

James's goat's cheese and courgette salad works as a starter for a relaxed dinner party with friends, or as a lovely light summer supper.

Preheat the grill to high.

Heat a griddle pan until searing hot. Rub the courgette slices with the olive oil and season with salt and freshly ground black pepper.

Place the courgettes on the griddle and cook for a minute on each side until marked with griddle lines. Remove from the griddle and top with a slice of the goat's cheese.

Place the courgette and goat's cheese under the grill and cook for 1–2 minutes until the cheese has melted and turned light golden-brown.

Meanwhile, bring a pan of salted water to the boil, add the pea pods, broad beans and asparagus and cook for 2 minutes until just tender. Drain and set aside.

Whisk the sherry vinegar, Dijon mustard and extra virgin olive oil together with a pinch of salt, pepper and sugar.

To serve, place the radishes, shallot rings, rocket, spinach, watercress leaves and pea shoots in a bowl and toss to combine.

Gently open the pea pods, leaving them half open, and add along with the broad beans and asparagus, then toss lightly once more.

Lay the salad onto plates, then carefully place a couple of pieces of courgette on top of each and serve immediately.

Tip: Look for firm summer courgettes with vibrant-coloured, shiny, unblemished skin. James favours the dark green, tennis ball-sized variety for this dish, but the conventional kind will work too. Just remember, the harder and smaller they are, the better the flavour.

Serves 4

2 large courgettes, cut into 1cm thick slices
1 tbsp olive oil
400g good-quality goat's cheese, cut into 1cm thick slices
200g fresh peas, in pods
200g double-podded broad beans
12 spears asparagus, trimmed
1 tbsp sherry vinegar
1 tsp Dijon mustard
6 tbsp extra virgin olive oil
1 pinch caster sugar
4 large radishes, very finely sliced
1 banana shallot, very finely sliced into rings
50g rocket leaves
50g baby spinach leaves
50g watercress, leaves picked
1 punnet pea shoots
sea salt and freshly ground black pepper

Summer

Two tapas recipes

José Pizarro

José's tapas dishes can be served as appetizers, or eaten together as a meal on their own. The braised peas without the egg would make a lovely side dish with a piece of simply grilled chicken or fish.

Deep-fried chicken wings al ajillo

Cut the pointy tips from each chicken wing and discard. Dry the wings well on kitchen paper.

Cook in a deep-fat fryer or shallow-fry in a big frying pan filled with 2.5cm oil and heated to 180°C (or until a cube of white bread, when dropped in, turns light golden brown in about 1 minute). Add a quarter of the chicken wings and cook for 6–7 minutes, turning all the time, until cooked through, crisp and golden.

Meanwhile, for the dressing, put the garlic cloves on a board, sprinkle with some salt and crush them into a smooth paste with the blade of a large knife.

Put the extra virgin olive oil and the garlic in a small pan and place it over a medium-low heat. As soon as the garlic begins to sizzle, add the crushed dried chillies and cook very gently for about 2 minutes, until the garlic is very lightly golden. Stir in the pimentón and sherry vinegar and remove from the heat.

As soon as the first batch of chicken wings is cooked, drain them briefly on kitchen paper, tip them into a serving bowl and drizzle with some of the warm garlic and chilli dressing. Toss well together, sprinkle with a little sea salt and serve hot. Repeat with the remaining wings.

Serves 4–6

16 large, meaty chicken
   wings
olive or sunflower oil, for
   deep-frying
4 fat garlic cloves, peeled
4 tbsp extra virgin olive oil
1 tsp crushed dried chillies
1 tsp sweet pimentón
3 tsp sherry vinegar
sea salt

Braised peas and ham with eggs

Heat the olive oil in a medium frying pan. Add the shallots and garlic, cover, and cook gently for 5 minutes until soft, but not browned. Stir in the ham and cook for 5 minutes until golden brown. You can bake this recipe in individual small dishes as well.

Stir in the peas and chicken stock, partially cover, and simmer gently for 5 minutes until the peas are tender and the liquid has reduced to leave them just moist. Season to taste with salt and pepper.

Break the eggs, spaced well apart, on top of the peas, season lightly and cover the pan with a tight-fitting lid.

Leave to cook gently for 5 minutes, or until the eggs are set to your liking. Eat with some crusty fresh bread.

Serves 4

6 tbsp olive oil
200g shallots, finely chopped
8 garlic cloves, thinly sliced
900g fresh or frozen peas
200ml chicken stock
   (page 214)
150g thinly sliced Serrano
   ham, finely shredded
4 extra-large eggs
sea salt and freshly ground
   black pepper

Summer

Light summer broth with a herb dressing

Mark Sargeant

This simple chicken broth will sustain, nourish and delight. It's light enough for summer and served with plenty of mixed fresh beans, minted potatoes and a tangy herb dressing, it really wakes up the taste buds.

For the broth, place the chicken in a large pan with the thyme, bay leaves and stock cube and cover with cold water. Bring to the boil and skim off any scum that rises to the surface, then season with sea salt.

Place the potatoes and whole sprigs of mint in a large saucepan with water, bring to the boil and cook for 10–15 minutes.

Simmer the chicken for about 20 minutes, then add the courgettes, peas, broad beans and French beans. Bring back to the simmer and cook for 6–7 minutes or until the vegetables are tender.

Meanwhile, to make the herb dressing, place all the ingredients, apart from the olive oil, into a blender, then blitz for a minute or so just to break it down a bit. Pour in the oil and then blend again, this time until you have a smooth, bright green sauce.

To serve, divide the potatoes between 4 warm bowls. Add the chicken and vegetables: each portion should have a drumstick and a piece of thigh, plenty of bright green vegetables and some lovely broth. Spoon over some of the herb dressing and garnish the soup with the asparagus shavings.

Tip: Mark's herby green dressing takes no time to make and adds zing to roasted meats, grilled vegetables or fish. You can experiment with the herbs and add more or less oil depending on what you're using it for. Adding capers and omitting the coriander and Tabasco will give you the classic Italian green sauce, salsa verde.

Serves 4

for the broth
4 chicken legs, bone in, skinned and cut through the joint so you have 4 thighs and 4 drumsticks
1 sprig thyme
2 bay leaves
½ chicken stock cube
500g Jersey royal potatoes
2 sprigs mint
2 courgettes, diced
250g petit pois
250g podded broad beans, skin on
250g French beans, cut into 3cm pieces
sea salt

for the herb dressing
½ bunch flat-leaf parsley, leaves roughly chopped
½ bunch coriander, leaves roughly chopped
small bunch mint leaves, roughly chopped
½ lemon, juiced
1 garlic cloves, peeled
3 anchovy fillets
½ tsp English mustard
1 drop Tabasco
1 tbsp red wine vinegar
125ml olive oil
sea salt and freshly ground black pepper

to serve
4 spears asparagus, shaved lengthways and dressed in olive oil

Grilled lemon sole, cockles and samphire with garlic parsley dumplings and lemon sauce

Nathan Outlaw

Soft, garlicky dumplings and a creamy lemon sauce add a touch of luxury to this fish dinner. You can use Dover sole, or indeed any other flat fish, instead.

For the dumplings, preheat the oven to 200°C/400°F/Gas 6.

Score around the middle of the potatoes, then bake them in their skins for about 1 hour or until soft. Halfway through, rub the whole garlic with a little oil, then roast with the potatoes for 25–30 minutes until soft.

Let the potatoes and garlic cool slightly. Halve and scoop out the flesh from the potatoes (you need 300g). Push through a ricer or mash well. Peel the garlic, push the flesh through a fine sieve, then gently fold into the potatoes with the Parmesan, egg yolk, flour, lemon oil, parsley and seasoning, but don't overwork the mixture.

Bring a large pan of water to the boil. Place the dough on a work surface. Divide into 28 pieces, then shape into small balls (about half the size of a golf ball). Blanch, in batches, in the boiling water for about 2 minutes or until the dumplings rise to the surface. Remove with a slotted spoon and leave to dry on a clean tea towel.

Preheat the grill to medium-hot, place the fish on a baking tray and season. Place the fish under the grill and cook for approximately 10 minutes, or until the flesh comes away from the bone.

Meanwhile, place a pan with a lid on the stove and when the pan is hot, add the cockles. Add 110ml water and immediately cover with the lid. Steam the cockles for a minute, then drain. Discard any cockles that have not opened. When cool enough to handle, pick the cockles from their shells.

For the lemon sauce, whisk the egg yolk, lemon juice and zest together for 1 minute and then slowly add the olive oil in a thin stream, whisking all the time, to make a mayonnaise. Season with salt and pepper to taste. Whisk in the cream and add enough fish stock to thin the mayonnaise to a sauce consistency (you may not need all the stock). Warm gently over a medium heat – do not allow to boil. Taste and season with a little more salt if required.

(continued overleaf)

Serves 4

4 small lemon soles, trimmed
  and washed, left whole
500g live cockles
200g podded broad beans
300g samphire
1 tbsp chopped flat-leaf
  parsley
sea salt and freshly ground
  black pepper

for the dumplings

2 large baking potatoes,
  about 600g
1 garlic head
1 tbsp olive oil
1½ tbsp grated Parmesan
1 egg yolk
75g Italian 'oo' flour
2 tsp lemon oil
3 tbsp chopped flat-leaf
  parsley
sea salt and freshly ground
  black pepper

for the lemon sauce

1 egg yolk
1 lemon, zest and juice
200ml light olive oil
50ml double cream
110ml fish stock (page 212)
sea salt and freshly ground
  black pepper

Bring a pan of salted water to the boil. Blanch the broad beans for 1–2 minutes, then drain and refresh in cold water and double-pod. Bring another pan of salted water to the boil and just before serving, plunge the samphire into the water and cook for 2 minutes.

To serve, add the cooked cockles, samphire, broad beans and parsley to the sauce and bring to just below a simmer.

Place the cooked fish onto serving plates and pile the dumplings alongside. Use a slotted spoon to remove the cockles, samphire and broad beans from the sauce and serve alongside the fish. Pass the sauce through a sieve and spoon over the fish.

Tip: The dumplings on their own, or with a quick tomato sauce (page 217), would make a great, easy supper.

Cured grilled mackerel with pickled lemon, cucumber, broad bean and pea salad

Ashley Palmer-Watts

An elegant and refreshing dish, full of interesting, zesty aromas. Mackerel is a delicious fish, with dark flesh perfect for curing. Master the technique (which is easy), and you can play around with the spices and flavourings to suit your taste and whatever fish you're eating.

For the mackerel, first gently toast the coriander seeds and black peppercorns in a dry frying pan, then lightly crush.

Place the sugar, salt, lemon and lime zest, coriander seeds and peppercorns in a bowl and mix well. Spread the citrus cure onto a tray and place the fish fillets on it, flesh-side down. Cover with cling film and refrigerate for 2 hours. Rinse the fillets under cold running water to remove the cure, then pat dry with kitchen paper.

To make the salad dressing, mix together the olive oil and 110ml of the pickled lemon juice, set aside.

Bring a pan of salted water to the boil. Blanch the broad beans for 1–2 minutes, then drain and refresh in cold water and double-pod. Bring another pan of salted water to the boil, add the peas and blanch for 1–2 minutes.

Juice a third of the cucumber and reserve this for later. Peel the remaining cucumber and then cut the 4 sides off to leave you with a rectangular heart of cucumber. Cut the 4 cucumber sides into 5mm pieces and set aside.

Heat a griddle pan until very hot. Season the cucumber heart and drizzle with olive oil, place on the griddle and cook for 2 minutes per side until lightly coloured and soft.

Heat the griddle pan again until very hot. Lightly rub the mackerel skin with olive oil, place skin-side down on the griddle for 2 minutes, then remove.

In a hot pan, pour a thin layer of olive oil and add the cut cucumber pieces. Leave to colour on one side, then gently turn to colour further.

Reduce the heat, add the shallots and garlic and cook for 2 minutes. Deglaze the pan with the Chardonnay vinegar and reduce until almost all gone.

Add 4 tablespoons of the cucumber juice, the broad beans, peas and herbs

(continued overleaf)

Serves 2–4

for the mackerel
10g coriander seeds
1 tbsp black peppercorns
25g unrefined golden caster sugar
75g salt
3 lemons, zest only
2 limes, zest only
4 mackerel fillets, boned
olive oil

for the cucumber, broad bean and pea salad
125ml olive oil, plus extra for cooking
1 x quantity quick pickled lemons (page 217)
150g podded broad beans
150g podded fresh peas
1 cucumber
3 tbsp finely chopped shallots
1 garlic clove, very finely chopped
2½ tbsp Chardonnay vinegar
2 tbsp chopped dill
2 tbsp chopped flat-leaf parsley
2 tbsp pea shoots
sea salt and freshly ground black pepper

Summer

and heat gently to ensure the mixture remains moist. Season with salt and freshly ground black pepper.

Cut the cucumber heart into thick slices. To serve, pour the vegetables into the centre of a large plate and lay the grilled fillets of mackerel on top. Lay the pickled lemon and cucumber slices over and around. In a bowl, dress the pea shoots with the lemon dressing and place on the mackerel. Sprinkle with a little more lemon dressing and a generous pinch of sea salt.

Sprinkle with broad bean flowers if you have had the satisfaction of growing your own broad beans.

Tip: Look for cucumbers that are firm and rounded at the ends. Avoid any that bulge in the middle because they are likely to be filled with large seeds.

Oven-baked pollock with radishes, borage flowers and lardo

Tom Kerridge

Tom's idea of food heaven isn't fussy gastronomy, it's perfecting the old classics that everyone loves the most. The finishing touches on this dish lift it to new heights. Lardo is pork back fat cured with spices and herbs (found in good Italian delis). Here, it melts beautifully on top of the pollock, adding an extra layer of flavour. The dazzling blue borage flowers add a lovely garnish.

Sprinkle the pollock with a little sea salt, wrap in cling film, then place in the fridge for 2 hours.

Preheat the oven to 190°C/375°F/Gas 5. Rinse the fish and pat dry with kitchen paper, then cut into 4 portions and place in an ovenproof dish lined with a piece of buttered greaseproof paper.

Place the shallots, peppercorns and thyme in a saucepan with the white wine and the vinegar and simmer over a medium heat until reduced down to a glaze.

Add the double cream and bring to the boil, then reduce the heat and gradually whisk in 150g of the butter. Season with salt and freshly ground black pepper, pass through a sieve and keep warm.

Place a knob of butter on to each of the portions of pollock, then place in the oven for 3 minutes. Baste the fish with the melted butter and then return to the oven for another 3–4 minutes or until just cooked.

While the fish is cooking, wilt the radishes down in a frying pan with a little butter and sea salt, then set them aside and keep warm.

Heat the frying pan again until hot, add the remaining butter, the girolles and 50ml water and cook until the mushrooms are softened.

When the fish is cooked, spoon the butter sauce onto warmed serving plates, add the radishes and place the fish on top. Add the girolles and then place a couple of slices of lardo on top of the fish. Garnish with the borage flowers and serve immediately.

Tip: Some supermarkets now sell packets of edible flowers in the salad section. But you might want to grow your own borage. It is a self-seeding annual herb that thrives in British gardens, and makes a lovely addition to salads, soups or even a tall glass of Pimm's.

Serves 4

1.2kg pollock fillet, skinned and pin boned
2 banana shallots, finely chopped
10 white peppercorns
5 sprigs thyme
100ml white wine
100ml white wine vinegar
50ml double cream
200g cold butter, diced
10 radishes, cut in half lengthways with the tops still on
200g girolle mushrooms
8 slices of lardo
12 borage flowers, for garnish
sea salt and freshly ground black pepper

Summer

Roast sea bass with crab mayonnaise

Nathan Outlaw

Nathan says, 'Fennel always works well with sea bass: a little roasted or raw in a salad, then dressed with some orange juice, complements the sweetness and depth of flavour of the fish perfectly.' Buy line-caught sea bass, or the less expensive farmed bream, which is a similarly consistent fish with rich flakes of white meat.

Bring a large pan of water to the boil (big enough to submerge the crab). Season the water liberally with salt. When the water comes to a rolling boil, lower the crab into it and cook for 15 minutes. Carefully lift the crab out of the water, place on a board and leave until cool enough to handle.

Extract the meat from the crab (you can save the shell for the stock). Blend the brown crab meat in a food processor until smooth and save for the crab mayonnaise. Pick through the white meat, removing any shell and cartilage; keep cool.

Preheat the oven to 200°C/400°F/Gas 6.

Cut each fennel half into 6 or 8 wedges. Heat a non-stick frying pan over a medium heat and add a drizzle of oil. When hot, add the fennel wedges and cook for 2 minutes on each side until golden. Season with salt and pepper, transfer the fennel to a baking tray and place in the oven for 4 minutes.

Meanwhile, heat an ovenproof non-stick frying pan and add a drizzle of oil. When hot, place the sea bass, skin-side down, in the pan and season with salt. Cook until the skin starts to turn golden, then transfer to the oven to cook for 4 minutes.

When ready, take out the fennel and keep warm. Remove the fish and flip it over; it will finish cooking in the heat of the pan.

To make the mayonnaise, whisk the egg yolks, lemon juice and zest in a bowl and slowly add the oil, drop by drop to begin with, then in a steady stream, whisking constantly. Mix half of this into the white crab meat with 2 tablespoons brown meat, the chopped tarragon and salt and pepper, to taste. Keep cool.

For the sauce, whisk the cream into the rest of the mayonnaise and thin down with the crab stock. Keep cool until serving, then just warm through.

To serve, spoon the crab mayonnaise into the centre of 4 warmed plates, top with the fish and place the fennel alongside. Spoon the crab sauce around the fish. Finish with the orange pieces and a drizzle of olive oil. Serve at once.

Serves 4

1 live brown crab, about 1kg, placed in the freezer 1 hour before cooking
2 fennel bulbs, trimmed and halved
vegetable oil
4 x 200g filleted sea bass portions
sea salt and freshly ground black pepper

for the mayonnaise and sauce

2 egg yolks
1 lemon, finely grated zest and juice
300ml light olive oil
2 tbsp chopped tarragon
50ml double cream
110ml crab stock (page 213)
sea salt and freshly ground black pepper

to serve

1 orange, peel and pith removed, segmented and diced
olive oil, to drizzle

Summer

Linguine with red mullet, chilli and garlic

Angela Hartnett

Red mullet is such a flavoursome fish and cooking it this way shows how sweet and juicy it can be. Use a non-stick pan for cooking the fish so it doesn't stick when you come to toss everything together.

Bring a large pan of salted water to the boil. Add the linguine and stir. Cook according to the packet instructions until the pasta is al dente.

Heat the oil in a frying pan and sauté the chilli and garlic. Don't let them brown.

Add the red mullet to the pan and sauté briefly until cooked, then deglaze with the white wine and cook until reduced. Add the stock and cook until reduced again.

Drain the linguine and toss straight into the sauce. Add the lemon zest and the herbs, season with salt and pepper, and toss gently. Serve immediately.

Tip: Red mullet is highly perishable, so use day-fresh fish. If you can't find mullet, shrimp, crab or part-cooked lobster will taste just as good.

Serves 4

375g linguine
1 tbsp olive oil
1 red chilli, de-seeded, chopped
1 garlic clove, chopped finely
4 whole red mullet, filleted, pin boned and cut into strips
110ml white wine
110ml fish or vegetable stock (page 212)
1 lemon, zest only
2 tbsp chopped flat-leaf parsley
1 tbsp chopped basil
sea salt and freshly ground black pepper

Lobster with escargot butter

Tom Kitchin

The garlic and herb butter is usually served on escargot. Here it gives the lobster a rich and luxurious finish, offset by the briny sea flavour of the samphire. You can prepare your own lobster or buy ready-cooked for a Tom Kitchin classic with minimal effort.

If you're preparing the lobster, bring a large pan of water to the boil and add a handful of salt so the water tastes salty. Place the lobster in the boiling water for 1 minute. This kills it instantly and humanely.

Remove the lobster from the pot and leave to cool for 2–3 minutes before proceeding. Cut the lobster in half, starting at the head and working towards the tail. Remove the claws and submerge them in boiling water for 5 minutes. Leave to cool and then remove all the meat from the claws. Remove all the meat from the halved body as well as the coral and cut into bite-size pieces. Set aside.

To make the savoury butter, heat a large non-stick frying pan over a medium-high heat, then add a little rapeseed oil. Add the chopped Parma ham to the pan and cook for 2 minutes, stirring occasionally. Now add the shallots, fennel, mushrooms and garlic with the rest of the rapeseed oil and sweat for 3–4 minutes, stirring occasionally. Add the chopped herbs, stir well, then remove from the heat and let cool.

In a separate bowl, whisk the butter until creamy, then add the cooled vegetables and ham and stir to combine. Add the mustard, breadcrumbs, ground almonds and the lobster coral and mix well. Spoon the butter onto a sheet of cling film and roll the cling film round it to form a log. Twist the ends to secure, then refrigerate to firm up for at least 1 hour.

Preheat the grill to high.

Unwrap the savoury butter, cut into generous slices and add to the lobster meat and claws. Spoon the mixture back into the lobster body and grill for 5–8 minutes, until hot and bubbling.

Meanwhile, for the samphire, heat the butter in a medium frying pan. Once melted, add the samphire and cook for a couple of minutes.

Serve the lobster with the sprigs of samphire on the side.

Serves 4

2 whole lobster
handful fine salt

for the savoury butter
1 tbsp cold pressed
  rapeseed oil
25g Parma ham, finely
  chopped
50g shallots, finely chopped
50g fennel, finely chopped
50g button mushrooms,
  finely chopped
2 garlic cloves, finely
  chopped
½ tbsp finely chopped
  flat-leaf parsley
½ tbsp finely chopped
  tarragon
250g butter, softened
2 tsp Pommery mustard
2 tsp dried breadcrumbs
1 tbsp ground almonds

for the samphire
50g butter
400g samphire

Summer

Miso-glazed salmon, pickled cucumber and sushi rice

Paul Rankin

Marinating fish in a mixture of miso, alcohol and sugar is an age-old technique in Japan and gives the fish an intense salty sweetness and interesting character. In Paul's dish, the sushi is shaped into traditional 'onigiri' (rice balls or triangles), which means you don't need a rice-shaping mat: you can simply shape the balls in the palm of your wet hands. With a bit of practice, they will look perfect!

For the salmon, combine the mirin, sake and sugar in a small pan. Bring to the boil over a medium heat to dissolve the sugar. Add the miso paste, bring to the boil and simmer for 3 minutes. Pass the miso mixture through a fine sieve into a bowl and set aside to cool. Once cooled, coat the salmon fillets with the miso marinade, reserving some to coat the salmon again before cooking, and lay on a tray to marinate for at least 6 hours.

Meanwhile for the pickled cucumber, mix together the cucumber, chilli and trompette mushrooms and sprinkle with the salt. Allow the vegetables to stand for 30 minutes, then rinse in cold water and pat dry with kitchen paper. In a small pan, bring the vinegar with the caster sugar to the boil, then pour it over the cucumber mixture. Allow to stand for an hour, then add the pickled ginger. Drain the pickling liquor off the vegetables when ready to serve.

For the sushi rice, in a small pan, bring the rice wine vinegar, sugar and salt up to the boil, stirring to dissolve the sugar and salt. Once dissolved, remove the mixture from the heat and allow to cool. Wash the sushi rice 3 or 4 times in cold water and set aside in the colander for 30 minutes. Place the rice in a saucepan, then add 500ml water. Cover the rice and bring to the boil over a low heat. Boil the sushi rice for 12–15 minutes until the water has been absorbed, then remove the pan from the heat, keeping the lid on, and allow to finish cooking, off the heat, for 10–15 minutes more. Tip the rice into a wide bowl and fold in 4 tablespoons of the cooled rice wine vinegar mixture. When the rice is cool, use a spoon or scooper and use your fingers to shape into rice balls or triangles.

Serves 4

for the salmon
50ml mirin (sweet rice wine)
50ml sake
75g caster sugar
150g white miso paste
4 x 125g salmon fillets, skinless and boneless, any brown flesh removed

for the pickled cucumber
1 cucumber, peeled in stripes, halved lengthways, seeds removed and cut into 3mm slices
1 large red chilli, de-seeded, finely sliced
9 black trompette mushrooms, soaked and torn into strips
½ tsp fine sea salt
90ml rice wine vinegar
45g caster sugar
1½ tbsp Japanese pickled ginger, roughly chopped

for the sushi rice
60ml rice wine vinegar
2½ tbsp caster sugar
¾ tbsp fine sea salt
250g sushi rice

Summer

Once the salmon has marinated, preheat the oven to its highest setting. To cook the salmon, wipe any excess marinade off the salmon fillets and heat a dry pan until very hot. Sear the salmon fillets briefly in the very hot pan, then place them on a baking tray. Rub the top presentation side of the salmon with a little miso marinade and allow to dry for at least 10 minutes. Finish cooking the salmon in the oven for about 5 minutes until just cooked and still slightly pink inside.

To serve, warm the sushi rice in a steamer or microwave. Sprinkle the miso salmon fillet with black and white sesame seeds and place onto serving plates. Serve the pickled cucumber salad alongside with the sushi rice, sprinkled with a few sesame seeds. Garnish with herb cress and a sprinkling of seven spice pepper.

to garnish
black and white sesame
seeds, toasted
herb cress, such as rocket
or coriander cress
Japanese seven spice pepper

Harissa roast chicken with beetroot and halloumi salad

James Martin

This is just the thing for a relaxed supper with friends and family. The roast chicken tastes fantastic with a burst of flavour and chilli-heat from the harissa paste (a North African chilli paste), and served with a gloriously pink beetroot bulgar salad, it's divine. Harissa paste can add depth of flavour and spice to anything, from meat and fish to vegetables.

Preheat the oven to 200°C/400°F/Gas 6 and heat a large griddle pan.

Drizzle the oil over the chicken and season with salt and pepper. Place breast-side down on the griddle pan and cook for a couple of minutes, turn over and place on a large baking tray.

Put the chicken in the oven and cook for 30 minutes.

To make the harissa paste, heat a small frying pan and add the cumin and caraway seeds. Once they start to release their oils, put them in a small food processor.

Add the chilli, paprika, garlic, tomato purée and vinegar to the food processor and blend until smooth.

The paste will keep in the fridge for a couple of months if you cover the surface with a layer of oil. The flavour gets better over time.

Remove the chicken from the oven, spread over the harissa paste and place back in the oven for 10 minutes.

To make the salad, place the bulgar wheat and beetroot juice in a medium saucepan and cook for 10–15 minutes.

Reheat the griddle pan and oil the sliced halloumi with a tablespoon of the olive oil. Put on the griddle pan and cook for 1–2 minutes on each side until bar marks appear.

Place the cooked bulgar wheat in a medium glass bowl and add the cooked beetroot, pistachio nuts, herbs, pomegranate seeds, lemon zest and juice and the remaining olive oil and mix. Once the halloumi is cooked, cut into 3cm pieces and add it to the salad. Season to taste.

To serve, remove the chicken from the oven and allow to rest. Cut the chicken into pieces and place on a plate along with the beetroot and halloumi salad.

Serves 4–6

1 whole chicken, spatchcocked (ask your butcher to do this)
2 tbsp olive oil
2–4 tbsp harissa paste or shop-bought
sea salt and freshly ground black pepper

for the harissa paste (makes about 75g)
2 tsp cumin seeds
2 tsp caraway seeds
1 red chilli, roughly chopped
1 tbsp sweet smoked paprika
2 garlic cloves, peeled
2 tbsp tomato purée
3 tbsp red wine vinegar

for the beetroot and halloumi salad
125g bulgar wheat
400ml beetroot juice
65ml olive oil
150g halloumi, sliced
100g cooked beetroot, chopped
50g shelled pistachio nuts, roughly chopped
½ bunch mint, chopped
½ bunch coriander, chopped
seeds of 1 pomegranate
1 lemon, zest and juice
sea salt and freshly ground black pepper

Slow-cooked breast of lamb with slow-roasted aubergines

Anthony Demetre

Lamb and aubergine taste wonderful together. Add the salty bitterness of preserved lemons and the rich iron of spinach and they taste even better. Breast of lamb is a cheap cut with an amazing flavour, which is enhanced by long, slow cooking.

Preheat the oven to 150°C/300°F/Gas 2.

Smear the skin side of the breast with the garlic, rosemary, salt and pepper. Roll up the breast and tie with kitchen string so it resembles a Swiss roll, with the skin side outwards.

Heat a large casserole dish with a lid and add the olive oil and half the butter. Once hot, add the breast and cook until nicely golden all over. This could take 15 minutes or so; the slower the better.

Take out the lamb and set aside on a resting plate. Add the sliced onion, fennel seeds and herbes de Provence and cook for about 15 minutes until very soft. Place the lamb on top of the onion and add the wine, lamb bones and enough water to come halfway up the lamb. Lightly season the lamb, cover with the lid and place in the oven to cook for 2 hours. Lift out the lamb, remove the string and allow to cool. Wrap in cling film and chill in the fridge until needed.

Cook the remaining braising stock over a medium heat until the volume has reduced to about 200ml. Strain through a fine sieve, pushing out all the juices from the onion.

Preheat the oven to 200°C/400°F/Gas 6.

Place the aubergines on a baking tray and bake whole for 45 minutes, until soft and completely cooked. Remove from the oven and, once cool enough to handle, roughly tear the aubergine flesh, discarding the skin.

Heat a large pan and add the oil. Once hot, fry the onion and garlic until soft. Add the spices and dried mint and cook for a further 5 minutes. Add the salt and tomatoes and cook for another 10 minutes. Finally, add the aubergine flesh and cook for another 15 minutes over a low heat.

Serves 4

for the slow-cooked breast of lamb
1 breast of lamb, bones removed, but reserved

4 garlic cloves, thinly sliced
1 sprig rosemary, finely chopped
1 tbsp olive oil
50g butter
1 onion, finely sliced
½ tsp fennel seeds
½ tsp dried herbes de Provence
100ml white wine
sea salt and freshly ground black pepper

for the slow-roasted aubergines
800g aubergines, slashed
130ml olive oil
180g onions, finely diced
½ tsp garlic purée
1 tsp ground black pepper
1 tsp turmeric
1 tsp dried mint
1 tsp salt
1 x 400g tin chopped tomatoes

Meanwhile, for the spinach and preserved lemon salad, place the spinach and lemon in a large bowl. Put the olive oil, some of the juice from the preserved lemons, the balsamic vinegar and honey in a small bowl and whisk. Pour this dressing over the salad and toss together.

Just before serving, remove the lamb from the cling film and cut into 4. Heat a medium frying pan and add the remaining butter. Once hot, fry the lamb on all sides.

Serve kashk over the aubergine and finish with the chopped mint and coriander. Serve the breast of lamb (and jus) with the aubergines, spinach and preserved lemon salad and a little yoghurt dusted with paprika.

Tip: Kashk, or fermented whey, is traditionally made with the milk left over from cheese making. It delivers a rich umami hit and is a surprisingly useful ingredient, used to thicken soups, add flavour to stews, replace cream in chocolate making, or offset the richness of a roast. Find it in Middle Eastern grocers. If you can't get hold of any, a mix of sour cream or crème fraîche with grated Parmesan makes a decent substitute.

for the spinach and preserved lemon salad
100g baby spinach
4 preserved lemons, sliced
2 tbsp olive oil
½ tbsp balsamic vinegar
½ tsp honey

to serve
2 tbsp kashk (optional, see tip)
1 tbsp mint, finely chopped
1 tbsp coriander, finely chopped
2 tbsp plain yoghurt
1 tsp smoked paprika

Slow-braised pork belly with wilted greens, olives and capers and feta polenta

Maria Elia

'I love to cook pork belly this way,' says Maria. 'The bitter greens wilt in the unctuous pork jus, and if you make it ahead of time the flavours develop even further. Served with creamy polenta or mashed potato it's a match made in heaven – just think of those salty anchovies and olives!'

Remove the skin from the pork belly and cut the meat into 4 equal pieces, seasoning each with salt. Heat a little olive oil in a large heavy-based saucepan. Add the pork and cook over a high heat until browned on all sides. Add the wine and deglaze the pan. Transfer the pork to a resting plate.

Add the onion, leek, fennel, garlic and anchovies to another pan and cook over a medium heat for about 10 minutes or until the onion and leek are tender. Return the pork to the pan and add the wine from the deglazed pan. Add the chicken stock (this should be about 2cm short of covering the pork), then bring to the boil, cover and simmer for 1½ hours.

Add the greens, broccoli, capers and olives and stir to combine the leaves with the cooking liquor. Cover and simmer for a further 30 minutes, by which time the pork should be tender and the greens and broccoli wilted. If necessary, continue to cook the pork, covered, until the meat is tender (the time taken will depend on the thickness of the belly). Remove the pork and leave it to rest in a warm place. Add the lemon juice and season the greens to taste.

Meanwhile, to make the feta polenta, heat the milk, bay leaf, garlic and 400ml water in a saucepan until almost boiling. Turn off the heat and leave to infuse for about 20 minutes. Skim off any skin from the milk and fish out the bay leaf and garlic. Reheat until simmering, then add the polenta in a thin, steady stream, whisking continuously for 2–3 minutes until thick. Remove from the heat and stir in the butter and feta. Season generously with salt and pepper and drizzle with olive oil.

Serve the pork belly and vegetables in a shallow bowl with the polenta on the side.

Serves 4

for the pork belly

1.5kg piece of pork belly
dash olive oil
350ml white wine
1 onion, finely chopped
1 leek, finely chopped
4 garlic cloves, finely chopped
1 small fennel bulb, finely sliced
6 salted anchovy fillets
500ml homemade chicken stock (page 214) or shop-bought
300g mixed leafy greens, such as a mix of spinach, chard (red or green), kale, dandelion or similar, torn into rough pieces
200g broccoli, roughly chopped
50g capers, rinsed
100g pitted green olives, roughly chopped
½ lemon, juiced
sea salt and freshly ground black pepper

for the feta polenta

500ml milk
1 bay leaf
2 garlic cloves, bruised
150g instant polenta
20g butter
50g feta, crumbled
extra virgin olive oil
sea salt and freshly ground black pepper

Menu: Mezze

Forget the traditional three-course meal; an array of colourful mezze plates, followed by a sumptuous lamb stew, is infinitely more fun and a really sociable way to eat, with friends and family grouped around the table, sharing the variety of small tastes and sensations. Eat in the garden, if the weather's nice. And finish with James's walnut and pistachio baklava, if you're feeling greedy.

Starter

Vegetarian mezze by Angela Hartnett
(Grilled aubergine and feta; three bean salad with soft-boiled egg;
spiced chickpea salad) (page 87)

Main

Ottoman lamb with saffron and rosewater pilau rice
by Silvena Rowe (page 88)

Dessert

Walnut and pistachio baklava with almond and ginger ice cream
by James Martin (page 197)

Vegetarian mezze

Angela Hartnett

Angela's mezze-style dishes are simple, super-healthy and deliver big hits of flavour – sweet, spicy, salty – without filling you up too much. Simply add some chilled rosé, a dollop of thick yoghurt and a stack of warm flatbread.

Serves 4

Grilled aubergine and feta

Pre-heat the oven to 200°C/400°F/Gas 6.

Drizzle the oil over the aubergines and heat a grill pan. Place the aubergines on the grill and cook each side for 2 minutes then transfer to the oven for 4 minutes. Heat a frying pan and toast the pine nuts. Heat a clean pan, add the olive oil and gently fry the garlic, parsley and breadcrumbs. Add the pine nuts and golden raisins. Pour over the aubergines and finish with the crumbled feta and mint leaves.

2 tbsp olive oil, plus extra for frying
2 aubergines, sliced lengthways
1 tbsp pine nuts
1 garlic clove, finely diced
1 tbsp chopped flat-leaf parsley
2 tbsp Japanese panko breadcrumbs
1 tbsp golden raisins
200g feta, crumbled
whole mint leaves, to garnish

Three bean salad with soft-boiled egg

Add the green beans to a pan of boiling water. A minute later, add the yellow and runner beans. Boil them for 2–3 minutes until cooked to your liking, then drain and refresh them in cold water, then drain again and set aside.

In another pan of boiling water, cook the eggs for 7 minutes so that they are soft-boiled. Leave until cool enough to handle, then peel them and leave to one side.

Heat a small frying pan and add 1 tablespoon of the olive oil. Once hot, add the garlic and chilli and cook for 1 minute. Place the beans in a large glass bowl and finish with the rest of the olive oil and the vinegar, mustard and lemon zest. Add the herbs and spring onions. Serve with the soft-boiled eggs halved on top.

200g green beans
200g yellow beans
200g runner beans
3 medium eggs
3 tbsp olive oil
1 garlic clove, crushed
1 tsp sliced red chilli
1 tbsp red wine vinegar
1 tsp Dijon mustard
1 lemon, zest only
1 tbsp torn mint leaves
1 tbsp chopped flat-leaf parsley leaves
4 spring onions, sliced

Spiced chickpea salad

Drain the chickpeas and rinse them very well with cold water.

Heat the oil in a frying pan and gently fry the chilli, cumin and sumac until aromatic, then add the chickpeas. Fry for a few minutes, then combine with the other chopped ingredients and the lemon juice.

1 x 400g tin chickpeas
2 tbsp olive oil
pinch fresh chopped chilli
pinch ground cumin
1 tsp sumac
18 ripe cherry tomatoes, halved
2 spring onions, sliced
1 bunch parsley, finely chopped
1 bunch mint, finely chopped
1 lemon, juiced

Summer

Ottoman lamb with saffron and rosewater and pilau rice

Silvena Rowe

Silvena's slow-cooked lamb, flavoured with dried figs, spices and rosewater, is 'the gastronomic equivalent of having a massage in a Turkish bath from a large man with very soft hands' (according to our wine expert Peter Richards, at least). In other words, it's irresistible!

For the Ottoman lamb, mix together the honey, pomegranate molasses and warm water or stock in a bowl.

Dry fry the lamb rump strips in a pan over a medium heat. Add the honey mixture and more water, if needed, and bring to a simmer. Cook very gently for about 45–60 minutes until the meat is very soft and almost melting.

Meanwhile, place the minced lamb, cumin and chopped oregano in a bowl and mix well. Season to taste, and then shape into very small meatballs, about the size of hazelnuts.

When the lamb rump is very tender, add the meatballs to the pan with the figs, prunes and almonds. Season to taste and simmer for 20 minutes over a low heat. Add the sliced apple and, finally, add the rosewater.

For the pilau rice, gently melt the butter in a pan, then stir in the rice and cook for a minute or so. Add the remaining ingredients, reduce the heat and simmer gently for about 15–20 minutes until the rice is tender and the liquid is all absorbed.

To serve, pile the rice onto each plate and spoon the lamb alongside. Finish with a couple of sprigs of oregano.

Tip: For perfectly fluffy pilau, place a clean tea towel over the pan for 5–10 minutes as soon as the rice is cooked. This will absorb the steam and help keep the grains dry and separate.

Serves 4

for the Ottoman lamb
30g honey
2 tbsp pomegranate molasses
500ml warm water or chicken stock (page 214)
500g lamb rump, cut into 2cm thin strips
150g lean minced lamb
½ tsp ground cumin
3 tbsp oregano, finely chopped, plus 4 sprigs, to serve
200g dried figs, halved
200g stoneless prunes
150g whole blanched almonds
300g apples, cored and thinly sliced
20ml rosewater
sea salt and freshly ground black pepper

for the pilau rice
40g butter
200g basmati rice, washed and drained
200g whole blanched almonds
pinch saffron
30g honey
200ml light vegetable stock (page 212)

Autumn

To me, autumn means the arrival of many delicious ingredients in my kitchen. It's a season of vibrant colours, intriguing textures and incredible flavours. As we leave summer behind, my mind is always buzzing with different ideas for new and exciting dishes.

I've always been fanatical in my approach to seasonal cooking and one of the most thrilling things about autumn is the Glorious Twelfth on the 12th August – the start of the shooting season for red grouse, a species unique to Scotland. The game season is hugely exciting for me. I love the whole process – from collecting the animals, feathers and all, to plucking and preparing and eventually serving them in our restaurants.

Over the past few years, I have also introduced a special celebration-of-game menu – a tasting menu that includes various types of game, including partridge, woodcock and hare. I use every part of the bird, allowing our guests to sample and experience the flavour and joy of seasonal, glorious game. It's time consuming, but incredibly rewarding to follow the dish from beginning to end – the whole process really epitomises my philosophy: From Nature to Plate.

Being a chef in Scotland allows me access not only to game, but also to a host of other incredible local, seasonal produce. The season's root vegetables are a joy to eat and marry with autumn's game and meat perfectly. Some of my favourites include celeriac, wild mushrooms, beetroot and pumpkin. Their unique flavours really are delicious and I use them frequently throughout the autumn and winter months. I believe root vegetables deserve as much attention as the meat. They can be incredibly versatile and give me so many options in my cooking – ideal for soups, purées, crisps, vegetable gratins or simply roasted. The great thing about pumpkin and other seasonal root vegetables is that the flavours are all naturally in tune and marry together perfectly.

For those with a sweet tooth, there is an abundance of fruits that are delicious at this time of year. British apples, plums, figs and pears are at their best and, in my opinion, their sweet, fresh flavours are unmatched throughout the year. Make the most of them in pies, crumbles and tarts, which are truly comforting as the weather gets cooler. Fruits are even great when added to vegetable or game dishes as the touch of sweetness can really add another dimension.

Autumn is a great time for experimenting with your cooking. You'll be amazed at the fantastically fresh ingredients available at your local farmers' markets, butchers and greengrocers. Let all the natural flavours, textures and colours inspire you to cook up a warming, hearty seasonal feast – a true toast to autumn!

Tom Kitchin

Pansotti with ricotta, fennel tops and walnut sauce

Theo Randall

The great thing about this dish is that you can make the pansotti (or half-moon shaped pasta) a couple of days in advance. The combination of sheep's ricotta and fennel in the filling is light and delicious. The walnut sauce adds luxury and texture. If you have any sauce left over, it is very good served with tagliatelle.

To make the walnut sauce, crush the garlic with a pinch of sea salt in a pestle and mortar, then add the walnuts. Pound until smooth, then mix in the lemon juice, Parmesan, milk, olive oil and half of the parsley, one after the other. Work this mixture together so the sauce becomes emulsified, then check the seasoning.

To make the filling, beat the ricotta and fennel together in a separate bowl and season to taste.

Roll out the pasta dough in a strip 60cm long and 12cm wide. Place heaped teaspoons of the filling along the length of the pasta, leaving a 3cm gap between each one and making sure there is enough pasta free to fold over the filling. Brush between each portion of filling with a pastry brush dipped in water, then fold the pasta over and, using your little fingers, push down round each pile of filling to seal. Try to make sure that there is no trapped air inside or the pasta will burst during cooking.

Use a round pastry cutter around the filling, half on and half off the pasta, to cut out half-moon shapes. Pick them up individually to make sure each one is airtight. They will keep in a fridge on a floured tray for up to 2 days, or you can cook them immediately.

Cook the pansotti in a large pan of boiling salted water for 3–4 minutes, until al dente. Meanwhile, melt the butter in a large frying pan. Drain the pasta, add to the frying pan and toss together. Add a generous spoonful of the walnut sauce and toss again. Add a good grind of black pepper and serve, with extra walnut sauce and the remaining parsley.

Tip: The best ricotta is made from sheep's milk, as it has a much sweeter flavour and better texture than cow's milk ricotta. The shelf life of cow's milk ricotta is three times as long, however, so this is the variety you are able to buy in most shops. If you do see sheep's milk ricotta in specialist cheese shops, buy it and use immediately.

Serves 4

for the walnut sauce
½ garlic clove, peeled
110g shelled walnuts
½ lemon, juiced
75g Parmesan, freshly grated
2 tbsp whole milk
4 tbsp olive oil
2 tbsp chopped flat-leaf parsley
sea salt and freshly ground black pepper

for the pansotti
200g ricotta (preferably sheep's milk ricotta)
2 tbsp chopped fennel leaves or Florence fennel tops (i.e. the feathery top of the bulb)
½ x quantity rich egg pasta (page 222)
50g butter
sea salt and freshly ground black pepper

Pumpkin and Parmesan soup with roasted ceps

Bryn Williams

This soup has that salty-sweet flavour that most people love, as well as being beautiful to look at. With their sweet and complex flavour, squash are at their absolute best at this time of year. Serve on a cold day with crusty rolls.

Heat a large frying pan over a low-medium heat. When the pan is hot, add the butter and onion and fry gently for 8–10 minutes, or until softened but not coloured. Increase the heat to medium, add the pumpkin and continue to fry, stirring well, for 2–3 minutes.

Pour the vegetable stock over the pumpkin mixture and bring to the boil. Stir in the Parmesan rind and cheese, then return the mixture to a simmer and continue to simmer for a further 8–10 minutes. Season, to taste, with salt and freshly ground black pepper.

Transfer batches of the mixture to a food processor and blend to a smooth purée. Repeat the process until all of the mixture has been blended to a purée. Strain the soup mixture through a fine sieve into a clean saucepan and heat until warmed through.

Meanwhile, for the garnish, heat a frying pan over a high heat until hot. Add the pumpkin seeds and dry fry until toasted. Add the vegetable oil and continue to fry the seeds for 4–5 minutes, shaking the pan regularly, until golden-brown.

Heat 1 teaspoon of the olive oil in a separate frying pan over a medium heat. Add the diced pumpkin (for the garnish) and fry for 1–2 minutes, or until just softened. Remove from the pan and set aside.

Return the frying pan used to cook the pumpkin to the heat and add the remaining 2 teaspoons of olive oil. When the oil is hot, add the ceps and fry for 2–3 minutes, or until golden-brown. Season, to taste, with salt and freshly ground black pepper. Stir in the chives until well combined.

To serve, ladle the warm soup into 4 bowls. Sprinkle over a pinch each of the cooked pumpkin, diced Parmesan and ceps. Finish with the toasted pumpkin seeds, then drizzle over a little olive oil.

Tip: Freeze the rinds from your Parmesan: they are very tasty and a great way to add a savoury flavour to stocks, sauces and soups. Simply add the frozen rind to the pan.

Serves 4

for the soup
50g butter
1 onion, chopped
1kg pumpkin, peeled, seeds removed and reserved, then diced
800ml vegetable stock (page 212)
110g Parmesan rind and cheese, roughly chopped
sea salt and freshly ground black pepper

for the garnish
25g pumpkin seeds
4 tbsp vegetable oil
1 tbsp olive oil, plus a drizzle to serve
25g pumpkin, cut into 5mm dice
110g fresh ceps, cut into 1.5cm dice
2 tbsp chives, finely chopped
25g Parmesan, cut into 5mm dice

Porcini, egg yolk, celeriac and thyme
Ben Tish

Yes, we're asking you to deep-fry an egg yolk. But stick with us; coated in crisp breadcrumbs it makes a tasty vegetarian treat with smoked wild mushrooms, celeriac purée and thyme vinaigrette.

Place the diced celeriac in a medium saucepan with the milk and season. Bring to the boil, then turn down to a simmer and cook until very tender. Drain the celeriac, reserving the milk, and place the flesh in a blender with half of the milk. Blend to a thick purée. Set aside.

Heat the oil in a deep-fat fryer or medium-sized, tall-sided pan to 180°C (or until a cube of white bread, when dropped in, turns light golden brown in about 1 minute). Prepare a bowl of ice cold water.

Heat a small saucepan of water until boiling and then turn down to a low simmer. Drop each egg yolk into the water and cook for 2 minutes until just set. Now quickly transfer the yolks to the cold water to cool down.

Place the flour, beaten egg and breadcrumbs in 3 separate bowls ready for coating the yolks. Carefully drain the yolks and transfer to the flour bowl. Gently coat with the flour, followed by the beaten egg, and then lastly the breadcrumbs. Set aside.

Heat a griddle pan over a medium heat. Rub the porcini with the oil, season well with salt and pepper and add to the pan with the garlic. Once the porcini slices are cooked through and nicely caramelised, remove from the griddle and reserve.

To smoke the porcini, make sure you are working in a ventilated space. Place a medium pan over a high heat and add the drained smoking chips. On top of this add some scrunched up foil or metal baking rings to form a trivet and then a small colander or strainer.

When the chips start to smoke, add the porcini to the colander and place a tight-fitting lid over the pan.

Remove the pan from the heat and allow the porcini to smoke for 3–4 minutes, or until they catch the flavour of the smoke. Do not leave the mushrooms too long in the pan as they can turn acrid. Remove and set aside.

Deep-fry the eggs in the hot oil until golden-brown and crisp. Carefully remove using a slotted spoon and drain on kitchen paper.

To serve, spoon some of the warm celeriac purée onto serving plates and then top with the mushrooms and the crisp yolk. Finally, spoon over the thyme vinaigrette.

Serves 4

1 celeriac, diced
400–500ml whole milk (enough to cover the celeriac)
vegetable oil, for deep-frying
4 egg yolks
110g plain flour
1 large egg, beaten
110g Japanese panko breadcrumbs
400g cleaned and trimmed porcini (or king oyster) mushrooms, sliced lengthways into 1cm pieces
dash extra virgin olive oil
1 garlic clove, very finely chopped
30g oak wood chips, for smoking, soaked for an hour in water
1 x quantity thyme vinaigrette (page 216)
sea salt and freshly ground black pepper

Tubetti pasta with cockles, mussels and rocket

Gennaro Contaldo

Similar to a (tomato-based) spaghetti alle vongole, but made with mussels and cockles, which are abundant in Britain and a fraction of the price of clams. If you're after delicious, authentic peasant food, this is it.

Discard any cockles or mussels with broken shells or open shells that do not close when given a sharp tap. Rinse the rest under cold running water. Place in a bowl with salted cold water and leave for about an hour. You will notice the shells opening slightly. Rinse under cold water again.

Place the rinsed cockles and mussels in a large saucepan together with the wine, garlic, oil and parsley. Cover with a lid and cook on a high heat for 3 minutes, until all the shells have opened. Remove from the heat and immediately discard any unopened shells. Remove two thirds of the cockles and mussels from their shells, leaving the rest intact.

Meanwhile, bring a saucepan of slightly salted water to the boil, add the pasta and cook according to the packet instructions until al dente.

Strain the sauce for any impurities, return to the pan with the shelled cockles and mussels and cook on a medium heat until it reduces slightly. Stir in the saffron, tomato and chilli, then season to taste.

Add the drained pasta to the sauce and leave to absorb the flavours a little. Mix in the rocket and season with salt and pepper. Remove from the heat and stir in the cockles and mussels in the shell. Drizzle with oil and serve immediately.

Serves 4

500g fresh mussels, cleaned and debearded (instructions on page 110)
500g cockles (or clams), scrubbed
150ml white wine
1 garlic clove, peeled
4 tbsp extra virgin olive oil, plus extra for drizzling
handful of flat-leaf parsley, roughly chopped
325g tubetti pasta
pinch powdered or regular saffron
4 plum tomatoes, de-seeded and chopped
1 red chilli, finely chopped
handful rocket
sea salt and freshly ground black pepper

Tip: Tubetti are short, smooth tubes of pasta, similar in shape to penne, which you could use instead. Or substitute with spaghetti and clams for the classic Italian dish. For a store cupboard treat, canned clams would work as well.

Plaice and cider onions with tarragon and anchovy butter

Nathan Outlaw

'Plaice is one of those fish that doesn't get enough praise,' says Nathan. 'At its best, it is unbeatable in my view. It can handle all sorts of flavours – cider, tarragon, anchovy and onions, for instance!'

Preheat the oven to 200°C/400°F/Gas 6.

For the flavoured butter, put the softened butter into a bowl. Chop the tarragon and add to the butter with the chopped shallots and anchovies. Mix well until evenly combined and season with pepper, and a little salt, if needed, to taste. Shape the butter into a roll on a sheet of cling film, wrap in the film and tie the ends to seal. Refrigerate for at least 1 hour to firm up.

Put the olive oil, onions and bay leaves in a roasting tray, pour on the cider and cook in the oven for 20 minutes.

Season the plaice all over with salt and pepper. Take the roasting tray from the oven and lay the fish on top of the onion. Put the tray back in the oven and cook for 12–15 minutes, or until the plaice is just cooked.

Meanwhile, unwrap and slice the butter. Lay it on top of the fish and pop the tray back into the oven for 2 minutes. Serve the plaice simply with the cider onions and lemon slices.

Tip: To check the fish is cooked, make an incision into the thickest part and see if the flesh pulls away from the bone.

Serves 2

for the tarragon and anchovy butter
200g butter, softened
1 bunch tarragon, leaves only
2 shallots, peeled, finely chopped
4 salted anchovy fillets, chopped
sea salt and freshly ground black pepper

for the plaice and cider onions
50ml olive oil
2 white onions, finely sliced
2 bay leaves
200ml cider
1 plaice, at least 1kg, gutted
sea salt and freshly ground black pepper

to serve
1 lemon, sliced

Sole satay heart

Henry Dimbleby

Henry is on a mission to get kids into healthy eating and this Asian-inspired dish should entice yours to cook too. It's fresh, flavoursome and fast. It also involves wrapping all the ingredients in a large paper heart so the fish is baked in the oven en papillote, which means 'in parchment'. The satay sauce is quite rich, so serve with a bowl of plain rice and a simple lettuce salad.

Preheat the oven to 180°C/350°F/Gas 4.

To make the satay sauce, place the shallots, ginger, garlic (save for 2 cloves), turmeric, soy sauce, fish sauce and chillies, if using, in a food processor and blend. Heat a saucepan and, once hot, add the oil and gently fry the blended mixture until the oil starts to come out. Remove from the heat and stir in the nut butter and coconut milk. Leave to cool.

Cut out a 36cm long rectangle of non-stick baking paper and foil. Lay the paper on top of the foil. Fold it in the middle lengthways and cut out a large heart shape on the fold. Smear some of the satay mixture on one side of the heart and place the sole fillets on top, overlapping slightly. Spoon over the remaining satay mix. Top with the spring onion, red pepper and lime juice and fold the foil and greaseproof paper around the filling like a pasty, starting from the top of the heart and twisting all the way to the bottom (I go round twice for good measure). Bake in the oven for 15 minutes.

Meanwhile, heat a frying pan and add the cashews. Chop the remaining garlic cloves. When the cashews are lightly toasted, add a tiny bit of oil and the remaining garlic cloves and the chopped chilli. Transfer to a small bowl and allow to cool.

Put 300ml of water into a pan and add the rice. Bring to the boil, then cover and reduce the heat to very low. Cook for 10–15 minutes or until the rice is tender and all the water is absorbed.

To serve, place the lettuce in a large bowl and dress with vinaigrette. Place the cooked rice on a large oval serving plate and bring the wrapped fish to the table. Pierce with a knife and place the fillets of fish on top of the rice, spoon over any cooking juices and add a squeeze of lime juice. Top with the toasted cashews, garlic and chilli. Sprinkle over the chopped coriander and serve with the green salad.

Serves 4

for the satay sauce
2 shallots, roughly chopped
5cm piece fresh ginger, roughly chopped
1 head garlic, separated into cloves, each peeled
1 tsp turmeric
4 tsp dark soy sauce
good splash fish sauce
2 red chillies, de-seeded (optional)
4 tbsp vegetable oil
4 tbsp crunchy cashew nut butter (or peanut butter)
200ml tinned coconut milk

for the sole
2 skinless lemon sole fillets
2 spring onions, chopped into fine batons
½ red pepper, finely chopped
2 limes, juiced
2 tbsp cashew nuts, lightly crushed
dash olive oil
1 red chilli, de-seeded, chopped

to serve
200g basmati rice
1 iceberg lettuce, core removed, shredded
1 x quantity basic vinaigrette (page 214)
squeeze lime juice
good handful coriander leaves

Crab and chilli squid ink linguine
Angela Hartnett

A simple, colourful plate of pasta that tastes as vibrant as it looks. It's easy to make Angela's squid ink pasta in a food processor and squid ink can be found at your fishmonger, but, you could also buy a packet of squid ink pasta or use a good-quality plain linguine, which works well too.

To make the pasta, place the eggs, yolks and squid ink in a medium bowl and whisk to combine. Place the flour in a food processor and add the liquid until it forms a dough.

Tip the dough onto a lightly floured surface, gather it into a ball and knead with the heel of your hand for a few minutes, until smooth and elastic. Wrap in cling film and chilll in the fridge for 30 minutes.

Cut the dough into quarters, put one quarter onto a lightly floured surface, and cover the rest with a clean, damp cloth to prevent it drying out. Shape the dough into a rectangle, flattening it with your hands so it fits through the pasta machine rollers. Lightly flour the pasta machine rollers, then feed the dough through on the widest setting and onto the floured surface. Continue to feed the dough through the machine, reducing the width of the rollers each time, until you are on the narrowest setting. Cover with the damp cloth and repeat with the remaining dough to give you 4 long strips.

Once the pasta sheets have reached the ideal thickness, use the cutters on your machine to cut it into linguine. Place the cut pasta on a long tray in a single layer, dusting with semolina so it doesn't stick. Place on a plate in the fridge until needed.

For the crab and chilli, heat the olive oil in a large, deep-frying pan and add the garlic, spring onions, chilli and ginger. Fry lightly without colouring for 1 minute. Stir in the crab meat and heat through for another minute. Add the wine to the pan and allow to bubble and reduce completely.

Meanwhile, bring a large pan of salted water to the boil and cook the linguine for 1–2 minutes if fresh, or according to packet instructions, until al dente. Drain the pasta and add to the crab. Stir in the parsley and basil and toss everything together to coat evenly. Season to taste and serve immediately.

Tip: If you don't have a pasta machine, roll by hand. Cut the dough in half and roll it half at a time on a lightly floured board until it's as thin as you want it. This is quite difficult because the dough is so stiff, but it is possible. Trim to the size you need.

Serves 4

for the squid ink pasta
2 eggs
3 egg yolks
3 sachets squid ink
250g Italian 'oo' flour
fine semolina (durum wheat) flour, for dusting

for the crab and chilli
2 tbsp olive oil
1 garlic clove, finely chopped
4 spring onions, finely sliced
1 red chilli, de-seeded, finely chopped
2cm piece fresh ginger, peeled, finely chopped
200g white crab meat
25ml white wine
1 tbsp chopped flat-leaf parsley
1 tbsp chopped basil
sea salt and freshly ground black pepper

Autumn

Squid pie with fennel and mint salad
Stéphane Reynaud

Stéphane's rich and rustic pie goes beautifully with the bright, sharp flavours of the light fennel and mint salad. Lavish a bit of love on this dish by making your own shortcrust pastry (page 226) or make it super-simple with some shop-bought stuff.

Preheat the oven to 180°C/350°F/Gas 4.

In a heavy frying pan, gently sauté the squid with the celery, onions and garlic in 30ml of the olive oil. Add the white wine, tomatoes, black olives and sugar. Cook over a low heat for 1 hour – the mixture needs to stew together well. Allow to cool and season. Combine the paprika with the remaining olive oil and set aside.

Divide the pastry in half and roll out 2 rounds, about 3mm thick, making sure one round is slightly larger than the other. Line a baking tray with non-stick baking paper and lay the smaller round of pastry on top. Spread the squid mixture over the pastry, leaving a 1cm border all around. Glaze the edges with the beaten egg yolk. Cover with the second piece of pastry. Seal the 2 rounds of pastry dough together by pinching the edges, and then roll them inwards so they stick together.

Brush the pie with the paprika oil and bake for 30 minutes until golden.

To make the salad, place the sliced fennel and mint leaves in a medium-sized bowl. In a small bowl, whisk the lemon zest and juice with the oil. Pour the dressing over the fennel and mint and mix together.

To serve, place the pie on a serving board and pile the salad next to it.

Tip: For ready-made pastry, look out for an all-butter supermarket own brand. Buy the unrolled blocks of pastry rather than ready-rolled sheets.

Serves 4

500g squid, prepared, tentacles reserved and squid cut into thin rings (ask your fishmonger to do this)
½ stick celery, sliced
2 small onions, finely chopped
3 garlic cloves, finely chopped
40ml olive oil
75ml dry white wine
500g tomatoes, skin and seeds removed, roughly chopped
25g pitted black olives, whole or chopped
¾ tbsp light brown sugar
1½ tsp paprika
250g pâte brisée (shortcrust pastry – page 226) or 1 packet all-butter shortcrust pastry
1 egg yolk, lightly beaten
sea salt and freshly ground black pepper

for the fennel and mint salad
2 fennel bulbs, thinly sliced
½ bunch mint, leaves only
1 lemon, zest and juice
3 tbsp olive oil

Keralan seafood pie

Vivek Singh

Inspired by the signature 'moily' of Kerala in Southern India – a very simple fish curry made with coconut milk, curry leaves, green chillies and ginger – Vivek's pie uses fewer ingredients and spices than many Indian recipes, but relies on day-fresh seafood for the beauty of the dish to be fully appreciated.

Preheat the oven to 200°C/400°F/Gas 6.

For the sauce, heat the oil in a large frying pan, add the curry leaves, the onion, ginger and green chillies and cook, stirring, for 6–8 minutes, until the onion is translucent. Add the turmeric, followed by the rice flour, stirring to mix evenly. Add the thick coconut milk and salt.

Discard any mussels with broken shells or open shells that do not close when given a sharp tap. Add the rest to the sauce and simmer for 2–3 minutes, until the mussels open up and the sauce begins to turn glossy. Remove the mussels from the pan and discard any mussels that haven't opened. Remove the remainder from their shells and set aside, discarding the shells. Continue simmering the sauce until very thick. Remove from the heat and set aside. When cool, stir in the shelled mussels and other seafood.

Roll the puff pastry into four 16cm circles, each about 3mm thick. The pies need to be cooked as briefly as possible, so roll the pastry as thinly as you can to help reduce the cooking time, otherwise the fish will overcook.

Divide the seafood mixture among 4 shallow cast-iron skillets or ovenproof dishes and sprinkle each pie with a couple of curry leaves and half a green chilli.

Cover each skillet with a puff pastry circle, brush with the egg glaze and sprinkle with the black mustard seeds. Bake in the preheated oven for 10–12 minutes, until the pastry is crisp and golden.

Meanwhile, make the salad. Place the sprouted seeds and bean sprouts, the tomato, green chillies, if using, and cucumber in a mixing bowl.

Whisk together the olive oil, lemon juice, salt and sugar to make a dressing and combine it with the diced ingredients. Serve with the pies.

Serves 4

for the seafood
500g fresh mussels, cleaned and debearded
250g raw prawns, shelled, de-veined
200g undyed smoked haddock fillet, cut into 2.5cm dice
200g squid tubes or cuttlefish, cleaned and scored
500g all-butter puff pastry
8 fresh curry leaves
2 green chillies, slit lengthways
1 egg, beaten, to glaze
black mustard seeds, to garnish

for the sauce
2 tbsp coconut oil or vegetable oil
12 fresh curry leaves
1 large onion, sliced
2.5cm piece fresh ginger, cut into fine strips
6 green chillies, slit lengthways
½ tsp turmeric

1½ tsp rice flour
500ml extra-thick coconut
    milk (if using tinned milk,
    separate the thick milk
    from the thin)
1 tsp salt

for the salad
100g sprouted fenugreek
    seeds (page 218)
100g bean sprouts
1 tomato, de-seeded, cut into
    5mm dice
1 green chilli, finely chopped
    (optional)
½ cucumber, de-seeded, cut
    into 5mm dice
2 tbsp olive oil
½ lemon, juiced
½ tsp salt
½ tsp sugar

Tip: To clean the mussels, plunge them in a basin of cold, running water, scrubbing the shells well or rubbing them briskly against each other to get them nice and clean. Pull off the hairy 'beards'. Don't let them stand in water – they will open and lose their natural juices.

Autumn

Roast masala chicken and masala potatoes

Madhur Jaffrey

The perfect Sunday roast for any curry lover – the chilli and citrus marinade makes the meat really juicy and full of flavour. And the spicy masala potatoes zing!

Preheat the oven to 200°C/400°F/Gas 6.

Place all the marinade ingredients into a blender and process to a paste.

Using a sharp knife, make 2 deep, diagonal cuts into each breast of the chicken, going all the way down to the bone. Make 2 equally deep slashes in the thighs and 2 in the drumsticks as well.

Place the chicken, breast-side up, on a roasting tray lined with enough foil to cover the bird completely. Pour the marinade paste over the chicken, rubbing it well into all the cuts. Set aside for 30 minutes.

Sprinkle the chilli powder and black pepper over the chicken evenly. Wrap up the chicken in the foil so it is completely covered, with the tightly closed seam at the top. Bake in the middle of the preheated oven for 1 hour.

Meanwhile, for the roasted masala potatoes, pour the oil into a large bowl. Add the potatoes and sprinkle in the salt and pepper. Ensure the potatoes are well coated, then transfer to a baking tray in a single layer.

Unwrap the chicken, without letting the juices run out, and return to the oven to cook, uncovered, for 15 minutes, basting 2 or 3 times with the juices. Place the potatoes in the middle of the oven at the same time and roast for 20 minutes.

Check the chicken is cooked by inserting a skewer into the thickest part of the thigh, between the leg and the body. If the juices run clear with no trace of pink, it is cooked. Continue to cook for a little longer if needed. Set the chicken in a warm place to rest for 10–15 minutes.

Lower the oven temperature to 180°C/350°F/Gas 4. Spoon the coriander, cumin, turmeric and chilli powder onto a plate and mix well. Remove the potatoes from the oven. Using tongs, roll the potatoes in the spice mix, making sure all sides are covered. Return them to the oven for a further 20 minutes, or until lightly browned and tender all the way through when pierced with a knife.

Carve the chicken, garnish with lemon, green chilli and coriander sprigs and serve with the roasted masala potatoes.

Serves 4–6

for the marinade
4 tbsp lemon juice
2 tbsp peeled, finely chopped fresh ginger
2 tbsp finely chopped garlic
3 hot green chillies, finely chopped
1 tsp salt
1 tsp ground coriander
1 tsp garam masala

for the chicken
1.75kg whole chicken, skinned
½ tsp chilli powder
½ tsp freshly ground black pepper
lemon slices or wedges, to garnish
sliced green chillies, to garnish
coriander sprigs, to garnish

for the roasted masala potatoes
6 tbsp olive or sunflower oil
5 medium potatoes, peeled, halved lengthways, cut into 5 x 4cm chunks
¾ tsp salt
¾ tsp freshly coarse-ground black pepper
1 tsp ground coriander
1 tsp ground cumin
½ tsp turmeric
1 tsp Kashmiri (mild) chilli powder

Spicy chicken Calabrese with olive oil mash

Francesco Mazzei

Francesco's rustic chicken stew is the perfect all-in-one-dish. It's fresh, warming and the kind of thing a mama would cook for you in Calabria, where they like food spicy!

Preheat the oven to 180°C/350°F/Gas 4.

Place the flour in a bowl and season with salt and freshly ground black pepper. Lightly coat the chicken thighs in the seasoned flour. Heat the oil in a large frying pan over a medium heat and add the chicken, cooking until golden brown on all sides.

In a separate ovenproof pan, gently fry the shallots and 'nduja for a few minutes. Add the chopped peppers, passata and 200ml chicken stock. Bring to the boil before adding the cooked chicken, chilli and chopped herbs. Remove from the heat, taste for seasoning, and add salt and freshly ground pepper, to taste.

Transfer the pan to the oven and bake for approximately 20 minutes.

Meanwhile, for the mash, place the potatoes in a large saucepan and cover with water. Add a pinch of salt and bring to the boil. Simmer for 10–15 minutes until tender. Drain well and return to the dry pan for a few seconds to steam and dry off a little.

Mash well using a potato masher, gradually adding the olive oil as you go, then season generously with salt and pepper.

Place a bed of olive oil mashed potatoes on each plate and top with a couple of the chicken pieces. Serve hot.

Tip: 'Nduja is a fiery, spreadable salami, loved by chefs for its intense flavour and versatility. A few pieces will transform a pizza margherita or a simple tomato sauce. If you can't find any, this recipe still works really well without it.

Serves 4

for the chicken Calabrese
2 tbsp plain flour
8 chicken thighs
2 tsp extra virgin olive oil
20g chopped shallots
100g 'nduja (see tip)
6 peppers, 2 red, 2 yellow, 2 green, de-seeded, roughly chopped
100ml tomato passata
400ml chicken stock (page 214)
1 large chilli, finely chopped
small bunch marjoram, chopped
small bunch chives, chopped
small bunch flat-leaf parsley, chopped
sea salt and freshly ground black pepper

for the olive oil mash
1kg King Edward potatoes, peeled, cut into chunks
5 tbsp extra virgin olive oil
sea salt and freshly ground black pepper

Venison steaks with red cabbage and potato pancakes

Tom Kerridge

Red cabbage is a classic accompaniment to venison, but far too often it is stewed and loses its freshness. Tom likes to serve it with a crunch. There is plenty of acidity and sweetness all over the plate in this recipe, so the balance of flavours is very important. Taste everything as you go along.

Thirty minutes before you plan to cook, mix the red cabbage, sugar, salt flakes and juniper berries together in a non-metallic bowl and leave for the cabbage to soften.

Meanwhile, make the potato pancakes. Preheat the oven to 160°C/325°F/ Gas 3 and then turn it off. Mix the mashed potato, flour and baking powder together in a bowl. Whisk together the milk and eggs, then stir the liquid ingredients into the potato mix to form a batter.

Heat the rapeseed oil in a large non-stick frying pan over a medium heat. Drop a spoonful of the batter into the pan and fry for 2–3 minutes on either side until golden brown. Transfer the pancakes to the warm oven to keep hot. You should have 12–16 pancakes.

To make the clove sauce, bring the red wine, red wine vinegar, redcurrant jelly and cloves to the boil in a saucepan over a high heat, stirring to dissolve the jelly. Continue boiling until the liquid reduces to a glaze. Add the beef stock, return to the boil and reduce again by half to make the sauce. Pass the sauce through a fine sieve into a bowl to remove the cloves, then leave to one side and keep warm.

For the red cabbage, rinse the cabbage thoroughly under cold running water. Melt the butter in a pan over a medium heat, then add the cabbage to warm through. Do not overcook. The cabbage should still have a crunch to it. Keep warm until ready to serve.

For the venison steaks, melt the butter with the rapeseed oil in a large frying pan over a high heat until the butter just starts to turn a hazel-brown colour. Season the steaks with a pinch of salt, add them to the pan and fry for 3–4 minutes on either side until they are a lovely dark colour. Squeeze in the lemon juice and baste the venison with the pan juices. Do not overcook them, as venison has a very low fat content so the more well done it is, the drier it will be. Remove the steaks from the pan and leave them to rest, covered with foil, for 10 minutes.

Serves 4

for the red cabbage
½ red cabbage, shredded
150g demerara sugar
40g sea salt flakes
20 juniper berries, crushed
50g butter

for the potato pancakes
250g cold, dry mashed potato
75g plain flour
1 tsp baking powder
125ml milk
2 eggs
3 tbsp rapeseed oil

for the clove sauce
200ml red wine
100ml red wine vinegar
100g redcurrant jelly
4 cloves
500ml beef stock

for the venison steaks
50g butter
4 tbsp rapeseed oil
4 venison T-bone steaks,
    about 250g each
½ lemon, juiced
150g crème fraîche
1 tsp crushed Sichuan pepper
1 lime, juiced
sea salt

Tip: These potato pancakes make a versatile side, and are a great way to use up any leftover mash.

Whilst the steaks are resting, mix together the crème fraîche, Sichuan pepper and lime juice.

To serve, put a couple of pancakes on each plate, add some red cabbage and a steak, and then pour over the clove sauce. Serve with the spiced crème fraîche on the side.

Tamarind-baked back ribs with stuffed baked onions

Mark Hix

The trick here is to get the ribs nice and sticky so that the addictive sweet-sour flavour of the pomegranate molasses and tamarind penetrate the slow-cooked meat to give loads of flavour. Serve with the stuffed onions and a simple green salad.

Mix the tamarind paste, pomegranate molasses, garlic, ginger and cumin together in a bowl. Smear over the ribs and cover the bowl with cling film. Leave to marinate in the fridge for at least 24 hours (the longer the better).

Preheat the oven to 190°C/375°F/Gas 5. Line a roasting tray with a couple of layers of foil to prevent the cooking mixture burning on the tray.

Place the marinated ribs on the foil and cook for 30 minutes, basting every 10 minutes as they cook.

For the stuffed onions, wrap the onions in foil, stand them on a baking tray and cook with the ribs for about I hour, or until they are fairly soft. Remove from the oven, take off the foil and leave to cool a little.

Turn the oven down to 160°C/325°F/Gas 3, cover the tray with foil and continue cooking and basting the ribs for another hour. Remove the foil and cook, basting regularly, for a further 30–45 minutes. Remove the ribs from the oven and keep warm until ready to serve.

Meanwhile prepare the stuffing for the onions. Melt the butter in a frying pan. Season the pork mince with salt, pepper and ground cumin, add to the pan and fry over a medium heat for a few minutes, stirring, until lightly coloured. Add 125ml water and simmer gently for about 10 minutes or until the water has evaporated. Transfer to a bowl and leave to cool.

Once the onions are cool enough to handle, chop about 1cm off the top of each, keeping the onions intact. Scoop out the centre of each onion with a spoon, leaving a couple of layers of flesh to hold them together. Reserve both the onion tops and the scooped out flesh.

Finely chop the scooped out onion flesh and mix it together with the pork, breadcrumbs and parsley. Season to taste. Spoon the filling into the onions and replace the tops. Place on a baking tray, brush with oil and bake for about 30 minutes, until the onions are lightly coloured and the filling is hot. You can keep these warm for about 30 minutes or serve straight away with the ribs.

Serves 4

for the ribs
1–2 pork back ribs, about
    1.5–2kg
110g tamarind paste
110g pomegranate molasses
6 garlic cloves, peeled,
    crushed
60g fresh ginger, peeled,
    grated
½ tbsp ground cumin

for the stuffed onions
4 medium red onions, peeled,
    but tops retained
good knob of butter
80g fatty minced pork
2 tsp ground cumin
30g fresh white breadcrumbs
2 tbsp chopped flat-leaf
    parsley
a little vegetable or corn oil,
    for brushing
sea salt and freshly ground
    black pepper

Sausages in a red wine sauce with duchess potatoes

Brian Turner

The perfect dish for a chilly evening, made extra posh with a side helping of some old-school fancy mashed potatoes. Duchess potatoes should be golden and crispy on the outside and creamy on the inside: the trick is to use a fluffy, starchy potato, such as Desiree, King Edward or Maris Piper.

For the duchess potatoes, preheat the oven to 220°C/425°F/Gas 7. Arrange a bed of salt on a baking tray. Place the potatoes on the salt and bake in the oven for an hour.

For the sausages in red wine sauce, reduce the oven temperature to 180°C/350°F/Gas 4.

Heat the dripping in a ovenproof pan with a lid. Add the sausages and fry them to colour well all over, and then remove from the pan. Add the leek and onion to the pan and fry gently to colour them. Add the tomatoes, garlic, thyme sprig, bay leaf, wine and stock. Bring to the boil and replace the sausages, cover with the lid and place in the oven for 30 minutes.

Remove from the oven, take out the sausages and keep them warm. Remove the thyme and the bay leaf and discard. Heat the pan on the hob to reduce the sauce to a thicker consistency. Blend the sauce using a hand-blender and then pass it through a fine metal sieve to make it smooth. Set aside and keep warm.

Heat a frying pan, add half of the butter, 1 tablespoon of oil and the mushrooms. Fry until lightly coloured, then add the ham and fry to colour it too. Remove the ham and mushrooms from the pan and drain on kitchen paper.

Add the rest of the butter and the oil to the pan and heat. Once hot, add the bread and cook until golden-brown, then add it to the mushrooms and ham.

To finish the duchess potatoes, cut the potatoes in half and scoop out the middles, then pass through a potato ricer into a clean bowl. Beat in the egg yolks and apple purée. Season with a little nutmeg, salt and pepper.

Preheat the grill to high and line a baking tray with non-stick baking paper.

Serves 4

for the duchess potatoes
650g floury potatoes
enough salt to cover the baking tray in a thin layer
2 egg yolks
1 tbsp apple purée
grated nutmeg
1 egg
sea salt and freshly ground black pepper

for the sausages in red wine sauce
2 tbsp dripping
8–12 premium pork sausages
1 leek, finely chopped
1 onion, finely chopped
6 tomatoes, chopped
2 garlic cloves, finely chopped
sprig thyme
1 bay leaf
300ml red wine
300ml chicken stock (page 214)
50g butter
2 tbsp olive oil
100g button mushrooms, quartered
100g boiled ham, cut into 5mm batons
1 slice bread, crusts removed, diced 5mm thick
2 tsp chopped flat-leaf parsley

Tip: If you don't have a piping bag, just drop 12 mounds of the potato mixture onto a baking sheet and swirl with a spoon to create the desired pattern.

Put the potato mixture into a piping bag fitted with a star-shaped nozzle. Pipe 12 round mounds onto the prepared baking sheet. Beat the egg with a little water, brush over the potato mounds, then colour quickly under the grill for 6–8 minutes, or until golden.

To serve, share the sausages among the plates alongside the duchess potatoes. Pour the sauce over the sausages, sprinkle with mushrooms, ham and croutons and the chopped parsley.

Hand-made skinless sausages with pepper sauce

Antonio Carluccio

Antonio's motto is 'mof mof': minimum fuss, maximum flavour. And these rustic sausages fit the bill. They are a cinch to make (no machine needed) and are wonderfully tasty with this classic combination of fennel, garlic and chilli. Serve with some crusty bread to mop up the juices.

Mix the pork, chilli, garlic, fennel seeds and red wine together in a medium-sized bowl and season with salt and pepper, to taste.

Using your hands, divide the mixture into 12 and roll each piece into a sausage shape, roughly 8cm long and 3cm in diameter.

To prepare the sauce, heat a cast-iron griddle pan on the hob. Grill the peppers on all sides until the skins are black. Leave to cool a little, then peel away the skins and remove the seeds.

Place the peppers with all the other ingredients (except the oil) in a food processor and blend until smooth. With the motor running, slowly pour in enough oil to achieve a pouring sauce-like consistency.

Heat the oil in a large non-stick pan, very gently place the sausages into the pan and fry for about 10 minutes over a medium heat until golden on all sides. Serve immediately with the sauce poured over.

Tip: Antonio's grilled pepper sauce is endlessly versatile: use it as a condiment with grilled meat and fish, spread on crostini, or as a sauce for pasta.

Serves 6

for the sausages
1kg minced pork
1 tsp chopped red chilli
1 garlic clove, peeled, crushed
1 tsp fennel seeds
110ml red wine
1 tbsp olive oil
sea salt and freshly ground black pepper

for the sauce
2 large red peppers
2 large yellow peppers
1 tbsp salted capers, soaked for 30 minutes, drained
1 garlic clove, sliced
½ red chilli, finely chopped
5 anchovy fillets
olive oil

Menu: Harvest Feast

When the leaves start falling, it's time to celebrate autumn's bounty with food that's filling and feisty, earthy, sweet and seductive. Bryn's voluptuous starter and Tom's glorious grouse with roasted veg are full of big, robust flavours. To complete the feast, add a big hug of a dessert: Sat Bains's baked apple with spiced custard and apple granita fits the bill nicely.

Starter

Baked celeriac and crispy duck egg salad by Bryn Williams (page 125)

———————

Main

*Grouse with pumpkin, Jerusalem artichoke and beetroot
by Tom Kitchin (page 126)*

———————

Dessert

*Baked apple with spiced custard and apple granita
by Sat Bains (page 194)*

———————

Baked celeriac and crispy duck egg salad

Bryn Williams

*Sweet, nutty celeriac, slow-cooked until tender, dressed with truffles
and nicely cut by peppery watercress and a crisp, deep-fried duck egg.
A dish with punch and panache.*

Place the duck eggs in salted boiling water for 6 minutes, then drain and
refresh and place in ice-cold water for 30 minutes. Carefully peel the eggs.

Put the flour in a wide shallow bowl and season, add the beaten eggs to
a second bowl, then tip the breadcrumbs into a third bowl. Arrange in an
assembly line. Dip each duck egg in flour, then egg, then breadcrumbs,
then chill on a tray in the fridge.

Preheat the oven to 180°C/350°F/Gas 4.

Season the celeriac with salt and pepper. Heat a heavy-based frying pan
over a low-medium heat. Add the vegetable oil, followed by the celeriac,
and colour it all over. This will take about 30 minutes in all. You will need
to rest the celeriac on the side of the frying pan to help you get it golden
brown all over.

When this is done, add the butter and the thyme sprig, then place the
celeriac in the oven and bake for 20–30 minutes. Make sure you baste the
celeriac with the butter 2–3 times while it's cooking. Remove from the oven
and set aside on a plate to cool, then slice the celeriac as thin as possible.
Finely julienne a few slices and mix these with the mayonnaise to make a
basic remoulade.

Whisk the lemon juice, olive oil and grated truffle together with a pinch of
salt and black pepper to make a dressing. Dress the slices of celeriac with
the truffle dressing and a pinch of sea salt.

Heat a deep-fat fryer or pour oil into a deep, heavy-based pan to a depth
of at least 7cm and bring up to 190°C. Deep-fry the eggs straight from the
fridge for 1 minute or until the breadcrumbs are golden brown. Drain on
kitchen paper and serve, garnished with the celery and watercress leaves.

Serves 4

4 duck eggs
110g plain flour
2 chicken eggs, lightly beaten
110g breadcrumbs
1 medium celeriac, peeled
    with a knife
1 tbsp vegetable oil
50g butter
sprig thyme
3 tbsp good-quality
    mayonnaise
½ lemon, juiced
3 tbsp extra virgin olive oil
1 fresh truffle, finely shaved
    and 1 tsp grated
oil, for deep-frying
1 handful celery leaves
1 handful watercress, leaves
    picked
sea salt and freshly ground
    black pepper

Grouse with pumpkin, Jerusalem artichoke and beetroot

Tom Kitchin

Tom says, 'It may seem challenging to cook game at home, but my recipe is relatively straightforward. And it is worth every moment of effort when you taste the end result and relish the wonderful deep flavour and smokiness – a characteristic of game birds.'

Take the grouse out of the fridge so that they can come to room temperature. Preheat the oven to 180°C/350°F/Gas 4.

Place the beetroot quarters in a saucepan and pour in enough water to cover. Add salt and bring to the boil. Simmer for 30 minutes or until the beetroot is just tender. Then drain and set aside.

Meanwhile, peel the Jerusalem artichokes, cut them in half and immerse in a bowl of cold water with the lemon juice added to stop them discolouring. Cut the pumpkin into thick slices.

Heat a large non-stick ovenproof frying pan over a medium-high heat and add a little oil. Put the pumpkin and Jerusalem artichokes into the pan, season well and cook for 3–4 minutes, until they start to colour. Transfer to the oven and roast for 15 minutes. Cut the par-cooked beetroot into wedges, add to the pan and cook in the oven for a further 5 minutes.

For the grouse, turn the oven temperature up to 200°C/400°F/Gas 6.

Heat the vegetable oil in a large heavy-bottomed roasting tin. Season the grouse well, inside and out, and then sear them in the tin until golden brown all over. Add the diced vegetables, baby onions and thyme sprigs to the tin. Place the grouse on one breast and roast in the hot oven for 3–4 minutes. Flip the birds on to the other breast and roast for another 3 minutes. Pour the brandy into the cavity of the birds and place them on their backs to finish roasting – another 5 minutes.

Remove the tin from the oven and leave the grouse to rest for 10 minutes, out of the tin, breast upwards so the juices are evenly distributed. Remove the vegetables with a slotted spoon and keep all the pan juices.

Put the roasting tin back on the heat on the hob and begin to reduce the cooking juices. Add the chicken stock, bring to the boil and let the sauce reduce and thicken. Take off the heat, pass through a fine sieve into a bowl and keep warm. Once the grouse have rested, carve the legs and breast meat and put on a plate, then spoon over the pan juices and sauce. Serve the vegetables alongside with the hazelnut vinaigrette and top with watercress.

Serves 4

for the grouse
4 grouse, prepared and
   wrapped in bacon
2 tbsp vegetable oil
100g celeriac, chopped into
   1cm dice
100g carrots, chopped into
   1cm dice
100g celery, chopped into
   1cm dice
20 baby onions
4 sprigs thyme
2 tbsp brandy
500ml chicken stock
   (page 214)
sea salt and freshly ground
   black pepper

for the roasted veg
4 beetroot, quartered
8 Jerusalem artichokes
1 lemon, juiced
1kg pumpkin, de-seeded
drizzle of olive oil
good handful watercress
   sprigs, to serve
sea salt and freshly ground
   black pepper
1 x quantity hazelnut
   vinaigrette (page 214)

Autumn

Winter

Lots of people think that this is a time of year when it is hard to find interesting, fresh things to cook. But for a chef like me, winter menus write themselves. There are so many fantastic ingredients in season, and the challenge is to put all this brilliant fresh produce on the menu.

One of my very favourite dishes for this time of year is pheasant with cavolo nero and a chestnut stuffing (page 158) because, for me, winter is all about the kinds of strong earthy flavours you get from game and root vegetables – butternut squash, sprouts and chestnuts, even swede and beetroot. Roasted parsnips are one of my winter staples, and you can't go wrong with good old mashed potatoes. What better to go with the hearty comfort food that pies and stews offer for this wrapped-up time of year?

When I think about winter when I was growing up, it's always the game shoots that come to mind. Game is such a healthy and sustainable meat, and can be rich and hearty and delicate all at once. And I'm thinking not only of the pheasant that I cook here, but mallard, teal, venison, rabbit and pigeon.

But it's also not just about what you cook, it's how you source your ingredients, and how you combine them. Look for the freshest, wildest, but most sustainable produce wherever possible. That way you're not only doing the right thing by your taste buds, you're doing the best thing for the land and seas around us. Then consider the pairings of flavours and textures, what brings the best out of each element on the plate, and how different cooking methods and seasonings can transform the sorts of things that some people think are boring.

Spices like those used in the recipes here can transform a dish. So it's also a time of year to open up the store cupboard to discover the almost magic, secret ingredients that bring the best of seasons past and the promise of seasons new to the table. As well as spices, this can include ingredients like dried fruits, which can be revived using teas and flavoured waters for amazing taste combinations that bring dash to humbler winter fare.

And of course, it's a time for family and friends and celebration for all cultures, as the international flavours included here demonstrate. Great food is the essential ingredient in all that.

Broccoli and cauliflower cheesy leek bake

James Martin

A comforting dish, made even tastier by the addition of brioche crumbs and the earthy, nutty-tasting Lincolnshire Poacher cheese. The tenderstem broccoli and romanesco make a stunning side.

Preheat the oven to 180°C/350°F/Gas 4.

For the cheese sauce, melt the butter in a large pan, add the flour and cook for 2–3 minutes. Gradually add the milk, whisking all the time until it is completely incorporated and the sauce is thickened. Once you have a smooth sauce, add the mustard, Worcestershire sauce and grated cheese.

For the bake, melt half the butter in a medium frying pan, then add the chopped leeks. Cook for 2–3 minutes until softened, then add to the cheese sauce.

Melt the rest of the butter in a clean frying pan and gently fry the brioche cubes.

In a large pan of boiling water, cook the broccoli and cauliflower for 2–3 minutes and drain.

Take an ovenproof dish and lay the broccoli, cauliflower, cheese sauce and about two-thirds of the brioche on the bottom. Finish with a layer of the Lincolnshire Poacher cheese. Bake in the preheated oven for 20–25 minutes. During the last 5 minutes of baking, scatter over the remaining brioche and return to the oven to bake for 7–10 minutes, or until the brioche is crisp.

In a large pan of boiling water, cook the tenderstem broccoli and romanesco until just tender and drain.

Spoon the bake onto a serving plate and serve the broccoli and romanesco alongside.

Serves 4

for the cheese sauce
50g butter
50g plain flour
450ml whole milk
1 tsp English mustard
1 tsp Worcestershire sauce
200g Cheddar, grated

for the bake
50g butter
2 leeks, finely sliced
½ loaf brioche, cut into
    1–2cm dice
200g broccoli, cut into florets
200g cauliflower, cut into
    florets
150g Lincolnshire Poacher
    cheese (or other Cheddar-
    style cheese)

for the broccoli
150g tenderstem broccoli
150g romanesco (see tip) or
    cauliflower

Tip: Romanesco (often sold as romanesco broccoli) is an old Italian vegetable variety, with a crunchy texture and a flavour somewhere between broccoli and cauliflower. It is a light, vivid green in colour and amazing looking, with its fractal pattern of spiky, conical florets.

Mushroom quinotto

Martin Morales

Quinotto is like a quinoa risotto, but the method is a little different – the quinoa is cooked before being added to the remaining ingredients. Quinoa (pronounced keen-wa) is much healthier than white rice and the addition of wine, cream and cheese makes it just as indulgent as its Italian counterpart.

Rinse the quinoa thoroughly. Put it in a saucepan and cover it with the cold water and a pinch of salt. Set over medium heat and bring to the boil. Reduce the heat and simmer for 10 minutes, until all the water has been absorbed.

Meanwhile, put the olive oil and butter in a wide, shallow saucepan. Melt over a low heat and then add the onion and mushrooms and sauté until the onion is soft and translucent. Add the garlic and sauté for a further minute, then add the wine. Bring to the boil, add the cream and season with a grating of nutmeg and some pepper.

Bring back to the boil and add the cooked quinoa. Lower the heat and allow the quinotto to continue cooking, stirring constantly until it has the same thick texture as risotto. Add half the Parmesan, half the parsley and some salt, if necessary.

Serve with the remaining Parmesan, extra mushrooms and parsley sprinkled over the top.

Tip: Quinoa is gluten-free, easy to digest and can be used in the same way as rice in lots of dishes. Try it instead of rice in a stuffing or pilaf or use it to make a quinoa tabbouleh.

Serves 4

250g quinoa
1 litre cold water
1 tbsp olive oil
30g butter
1 onion, finely chopped
125g mixed mushrooms, finely sliced
3 garlic cloves, finely chopped
125ml white wine
125ml single cream
grated nutmeg, to taste
50g Parmesan, grated
4 tbsp finely chopped flat-leaf parsley
sea salt and freshly ground black pepper

Winter

Insalata di rinforzo
Antonio Carluccio

Carluccio's insalata di rinforzo translates as 'bracing salad'. It is a very simple dish to prepare, with easy pickled winter veg, anchovies, capers and black olives sharing the platter with a selection of cured meats. This is perfect sharing food, and traditionally served as the opener to the Italian Christmas Eve family feast.

For the insalata di rinforzo, put the vinegar, 1 litre water, the salt and sugar in a pan with the cloves and bay leaves and bring to the boil. Add the onions and carrot and cook for 10 minutes, then add the cauliflower and pepper and cook for another 20 minutes. Drain and cool.

To assemble, combine the capers, anchovies and olives in a bowl. Drizzle over the olive oil and add the chopped chilli. Mix all the ingredients well.

Add some of the pickle to the salad and combine.

To serve, place the sliced salami and prosciutto on a serving plate along with the salad. Any remaining pickle can be reserved in a fridge in a jar or served alongside.

Tip: This salad makes use of winter vegetables and, unlike most salads, any leftovers can be kept in the fridge and 'reinforced' in the days that follow with other ingredients like tuna, anchovies or eggs.

Serves 6

for the salad
1.5 litres white wine vinegar
50g salt
50g sugar
6 cloves
10 bay leaves
200g pickling onions
2 carrots, cut into small rounds
1 small cauliflower, cut into florets
1 yellow pepper, cut into strips
1 red pepper, cut into strips

to serve
30g large salted capers, soaked for 30 minutes in water, drained
100g anchovy fillets
100g black olives
4 tbsp olive oil
1 red chilli, finely chopped
12 slices salami
12 slices prosciutto

Serrano ham and chicken croquettes
Rick Stein

Serve these crisp mouthfuls as party finger food or as a starter. Rick says, 'The filling needs to be light and airy, which means serving the croquettes as soon as they are cooked. It also means making the béchamel filling as light as you dare, while still allowing you to roll them into a gobstopper and then a cork-shape prior to dipping them in flour, egg and breadcrumbs. Finally, cook them for no more than 2 minutes, until just a light golden brown.'

Melt the butter in a medium saucepan over a medium heat, add the ham and leave to cook gently for a minute or 2 to soften. Stir in 115g of the flour and cook for 1 minute, then very gradually stir in the milk, a little at a time, beating really well between each addition so that the mixture becomes silky smooth. Increase the heat slightly, bring to the boil, and leave to cook gently, whisking constantly, for 5 minutes to cook the flour.

Stir in the chicken and 1 teaspoon salt, or to taste, then stir in the hard-boiled egg. Scrape the mixture into a bowl, press a sheet of cling film onto the surface and chill in the fridge for at least 6 hours, but ideally overnight, until really firm.

For the croquettes, shape 1½ tablespoons of the chilled mixture between lightly floured palms into balls, and then cork-shaped barrels. You should make about 24. Refrigerate again for 30 minutes.

Heat a deep-fat fryer or pour oil into a deep, heavy-based pan to a depth of at least 7cm and bring up to 190°C. Put the remaining 75g of flour, the beaten egg and the breadcrumbs into 3 separate shallow trays or bowls. Take the croquettes from the fridge and dip them 4 or 5 at a time into the flour, then the beaten egg and then the breadcrumbs, then lower them into the hot oil and cook for not quite 2 minutes until crisp and lightly golden. You can tell when they are done because as they cook, the béchamel mixture starts to melt inside and the croquettes make a different noise in the fryer. Lift out onto plenty of kitchen paper and drain briefly. Serve while they are still hot.

Serves 8 (makes about 24)

85g butter
50g good-quality, thin slices Spanish air-dried ham, roughly chopped
115g plain flour, plus 75g extra for coating
500ml whole milk
75g cooked chicken breast meat, chopped
1 hard-boiled egg, peeled and finely chopped
vegetable oil, for deep-frying
2 eggs, beaten
200g fresh white breadcrumbs, made from crustless day-old bread left out overnight
sea salt

Tip: Once you've mastered the basic béchamel – or more correctly panada – for these, you can flavour them with pretty much what you like: chopped prawns, home-salted cod, (wild) mushrooms or grated, well-flavoured cheese.

Spanish fried salt cod, egg and cauliflower with a pepper sauce

José Pizarro

Salt cod, or 'bacalao', is a national treasure in Spain. Fried in a light flour and egg batter like this – crisp on the outside, falling apart in luxurious moist flakes inside – it's easy to see why. Jose adds fried cauliflower and egg with a piquant red pepper sauce for his tapas dish, which makes a very tasty, light supper.

About 24–48 hours before you plan to eat this dish, put the salt cod, skin-side up, in a bowl and cover with plenty of cold water. Cover and put in the fridge. You will need to change the water every 6 hours or so. To check if the cod is ready, i.e. no longer salty, take a little piece of flesh from the thickest part and taste it. You want it to be a little bit salty, but not too much.

Cook the cauliflower florets in a pan of boiling salted water for about 5 minutes, until just tender. Drain and place onto kitchen paper to dry.

Heat a deep-fat fryer or pour oil into a deep, heavy-based saucepan until about half-filled and bring up to 180°C.

Season the flour with black pepper, place on a large plate and roll the hard-boiled egg halves, cauliflower florets and drained salt cod pieces in the flour and then dip into the beaten egg.

Cook the eggs, fish and cauliflower in batches in the hot oil for about 4 minutes, or until golden-brown and crisp. Carefully remove with a slotted spoon and set aside to drain on kitchen paper. Keep warm until ready to serve.

For the sauce, first preheat the oven to its highest setting. Roast the peppers until the skin blisters and turns black. Remove from the oven, cover with cling film and leave to cool. Peel away the skins and tear the peppers into strips.

Place the olive oil in a medium frying pan over a medium heat. When hot, add the onion and cook for 2 minutes, or until softened. Add the garlic, saffron and bay leaves and cook for a further minute. Pour in the wine and allow to bubble for a minute before adding the stock and the peppers. Continue to cook for a further few minutes, or until the volume of liquid has reduced and the sauce has a thicker consistency.

Toss the fried cauliflower, fish and eggs in the sauce, divide among the plates and serve scattered with almonds and chopped parsley.

Serves 4

4 x 75g pieces salt cod
1 small cauliflower, cut into
  bite-size florets
sunflower oil, for deep-frying
50g plain flour
4 eggs, hard-boiled and
  halved
2 eggs, beaten
black pepper

for the pepper sauce

2 red peppers, quartered,
  seeds and core removed
2 tbsp extra virgin olive oil
  (preferably Spanish)
1 onion, finely diced
2 garlic cloves, finely sliced
1 pinch saffron
2 bay leaves
100ml white wine (preferably
  Spanish)
100ml chicken stock
  (page 214)

to serve

2 tbsp slivered almonds,
  toasted
3 tbsp chopped flat-leaf
  parsley

Alternative Christmas Menu

Christmas doesn't have to mean turkey and a day spent stressing over a hot stove. This alternative menu keeps things simple, but looks and tastes delicious. Kick off with a glass of champagne or Susy's sloe gin fizz (page 211) and finish with James's yule log for a festive feast, with plenty of surprises.

Starter

*Salmon gravlax with cucumber salad and horseradish mustard
by Aggi Sverrisson (page 143)*

Main

*Christmas porchetta with rosemary and garlic potatoes
by Gennaro Contaldo (page 146)*

Dessert

Chocolate chestnut yule log by James Martin (page 204)

Salmon gravlax with cucumber salad and horseradish mustard

Aggi Sverrisson

Gravlax is a traditional Nordic dish of raw salmon cured with sugar, salt and fresh dill. Aggi's version is a doddle to make, and uses very little salt and citrus zest for a light and delicate cure.

Mix the sugar, salt and lemon peel together in a small bowl. Lay the salmon in a shallow dish and sprinkle the marinade over. Leave to marinate for 1 hour and then rinse off under cold running water. Divide the fish into 4 portions.

Put the olive oil in a large frying pan and heat to 45°C (use a kitchen thermometer to check). If you don't have a thermometer, place the pan on the heat, then dip a spoon in after 30 seconds. Feel the spoon to check the heat of the oil – it needs to be just warm. Keep the oil on the heat and keep checking every 30 seconds until the oil feels warm. Add the salmon to the pan, turn off the heat and leave the salmon for about 15–20 minutes. Set aside to cool, then transfer to a plate and leave in the fridge until ready to serve.

For the mustard sauce, mix all the ingredients together in a small bowl and chill in the fridge until required.

For the cucumber salad, peel the cucumber and slice it into 1cm cubes. Mix with the vinegar, a little salt, olive oil and mustard in a bowl and set aside to marinate. Add the dill just before serving.

For the rye croûtons, drizzle the bread slices with olive oil and sprinkle with salt.

Heat a frying pan and fry the rye bread until browned all over. Remove from the heat and transfer to a plate to cool slightly before breaking up into rustic croûtons. Sprinkle with the chopped dill.

Sprinkle the chopped dill over the salmon and serve with the rye croûtons, mustard sauce, cucumber salad and mixed micro leaves, if you have them, to garnish.

Tip: In order to kill any parasites present in the fish, you can freeze it for 24 hours after buying and then defrost in the fridge.

Serves 8–10

50g caster sugar
50g fine salt
4 lemons, peel removed with a peeler, then finely sliced into julienne
1 filleted side of salmon, weighing about 800g, skinned and pin boned
600ml olive oil
20g chopped dill

for the mustard sauce

400g Greek-style yoghurt
2 tsp wholegrain mustard
pinch salt
20g muscovado sugar
2 tsp lemon juice
freshly grated horseradish, to taste

for the cucumber salad

1 cucumber
2 tsp wine vinegar
4 tbsp olive oil
2 tsp wholegrain mustard
10g chopped dill
salt

for the rye croûtons

4 slices rye bread
olive oil, to taste
pinch salt
4 tbsp chopped dill
2–4 tbsp mixed micro leaves (optional)

Christmas porchetta with rosemary and garlic potatoes

Gennaro Contaldo

Roast pork, stuffed with herbs, dried fruit and mortadella, with loads of crackling. Gennaro's porchetta tastes spectacular. And the best bit is that it's not hard to make. Ask your butcher to butterfly the meat for you, mix the stuffing and roll it up inside the meat and you're well on your way to the perfect Christmas dinner. You'll want to have a piece of string about an arm's length handy to tie your meat up once you've rolled it.

Preheat the oven to 220°C/425°F/Gas 7. Season the pork with salt and pepper and rub it into the pork, along with the lemon zest.

Place the Parmesan, pork mince, chicken livers, onions, sage, rosemary, thyme, bread, pine nuts and sultanas in a large bowl and mix.

Spread the filling on top of the butterflied loin and roll onto one side. Cover with 2 slices of mortadella and then roll halfway along. Pull in the other side of the loin, add the rest of the filling, then press down and put on 4 more slices of mortadella. Roll to secure and tie with kitchen string. Rub with olive oil and season with salt and pepper.

Place the whole carrots and onion, the white wine, Vin Santo and 125ml water in the bottom of a baking tray and place the pork on top. Cook in the oven for 30 minutes and then turn the oven down to 150°C/300°F/Gas 2 for 3 hours.

For the rosemary and garlic sautéed potatoes, heat a large frying pan and add the oil. Once hot, add the potatoes and cook for a couple of minutes. Add the rosemary and garlic and cook until the potatoes are crisp and cooked through.

To serve, place the pork and potatoes in the centre of the table and let people help themselves.

Serves 8–10

3kg pork loin, boned and butterflied (alternatively, use pork belly or shoulder)
2 lemons, zest only
15g Parmesan, grated
175g minced pork
175g chicken livers, chopped
150g onions, finely chopped
small handful sage leaves
small handful rosemary sprigs
small handful thyme sprigs
350g bread, soaked in 200ml water and broken into small pieces
15g pine nuts
30g sultanas
6 slices mortadella sausage with pistachios (about 200g)
dash olive oil
4 carrots
1 onion
250ml white wine
70ml Vin Santo
sea salt and freshly ground black pepper

for the rosemary and garlic sautéed potatoes
3 tbsp olive oil
1kg potatoes, peeled, cut into quarters
4 sprigs rosemary
6 garlic cloves, skin on, smashed

Tuna with parsnip and a shallot and pepper sauce

Stuart Gillies

The light, fluffy purée and parsnip chips add texture and a deliciously festive feel to Stuart's straightforward tuna dish.

For the parsnip purée and parsnip chips, heat the vegetable oil in a deep-fat fryer or pour oil into a deep, heavy-based pan to a depth of at least 7cm and bring up to 180°C (or until a cube of white bread, when dropped in, turns light golden brown in about 1 minute). Preheat the oven to 200°C/400°F/Gas 6.

Roughly chop 3 of the parsnips, place them in a saucepan and cover with 300ml water and the milk. Season with salt and a little sugar, to taste, and bring to the boil. Reduce the heat and simmer for 10–12 minutes, or until tender. Drain the parsnips well, then place in a food processor with a little of the cooking liquid and blitz. Place in a clean saucepan and add enough cream to create a smooth, creamy purée. Season with more salt and sugar, to taste.

Using a vegetable peeler, peel long strips along the length of the remaining parsnip. Carefully place the parsnip shavings into the hot oil and fry until golden-brown. Remove the parsnips using a metal slotted spoon and drain on kitchen paper. Sprinkle lightly with salt.

For the shallot and pepper sauce, place the red wine and shallots in a saucepan and bring to the boil. Simmer for 3–4 minutes, until reduced by half, then add the black pepper and leave to cool.

For the tuna, season the steaks with salt and freshly ground black pepper and heat the olive oil in a frying pan. Fry the tuna on both sides until lightly coloured.

Place the tuna on a rack on a small roasting tray and transfer to the oven to cook for 2–3 minutes.

Remove the tuna from the oven, turn it over on the rack and leave in a warm place to continue heating through for about 5 minutes. Leave the oven on. Slice each tuna steak in half diagonally at 45 degrees, turn each piece flesh-side up on the rack and then place back in the oven for 30 seconds. Remove the tuna from the oven.

To serve, place a large spoonful of parsnip purée in the middle of each of 4 plates and spread slightly. Arrange the tuna on top, flesh-side up. Spoon over the shallot and black pepper sauce and top with the fried parsnip.

Serves 4

for the parsnip purée and parsnip chips
vegetable oil, for deep-frying
4 parsnips, peeled
110ml milk
pinch of sugar
50–100ml double cream
sea salt

for the shallot and pepper sauce
150ml red wine
3 shallots, finely chopped
¾ tsp black peppercorns, coarsely ground

for the tuna
4 x 200g skinless (yellowfin) tuna loin steaks
dash of olive oil
sea salt and freshly ground black pepper

Winter

Griddled squid with sweet-and-sour dressing

Mark Sargeant

Mark's oriental squid is a great thing to prepare on the barbecue in the summer, but it's also lovely in the winter, when you fancy a light supper with extra zing. And squid is in season now, meaning it's inexpensive and sustainable too. Squid must either be cooked very quickly or for a very long time, otherwise it will be tough. Cooked properly, as here, it will be sweet and tender.

In a large bowl, combine the citrus zest and juice, herbs, soy sauce, chilli, grated ginger and sugar. Add the extra virgin olive oil and sesame oil and mix well until combined. Season to taste with salt and freshly ground black pepper.

Remove the tentacles from the squid and set aside. Place a flat wooden spatula inside one of the squid tubes, lay it on a chopping board, then score across the flesh at 5mm intervals with a sharp knife. Repeat with the rest of the squid.

Heat a griddle pan over a high heat until smoking hot. Meanwhile, rub the squid with the olive oil and season with salt and freshly ground black pepper.

Place the squid tubes scored-side down into the griddle pan and cook for 1–2 minutes. Remove the pan from the heat, flip the squid tubes over and leave for a further 30 seconds, or until just cooked. Remove the tubes from the pan, place in the bowl with the dressing and turn gently to coat.

Return the griddle pan to the heat and cook the tentacles for 1–2 minutes or until they start to crisp up on the edges. Transfer the tentacles to the bowl and turn to coat with the dressing.

Gently mix the watercress leaves with the squid and dressing and arrange on serving plates.

Tip: Preparing squid is easy once you know how: cut off the tentacles and remove the plastic-like shard ('quill') from inside the body. Keep the ink-sac to colour the dish later. Peel the purple and white skin from the squid meat. Remove the 'beak' from the tentacles (a small white piece of bone with a hole in the middle). The tentacles and squid body can be cooked.

Serves 4

1 lime, zest and juice
½ lemon, zest and juice
½ orange, zest and juice
1 small bunch coriander, finely chopped
1 small bunch mint, leaves finely chopped
1 tbsp dark soy sauce
1 red chilli, finely chopped
1.5cm piece fresh ginger, peeled, grated
pinch caster sugar
4 tbsp extra virgin olive oil
1 tbsp sesame oil
8 medium-sized whole squid, gutted, cleaned (ask your fishmonger to do this or see tip) and dried
1–2 tbsp olive oil
150g watercress, picked, to serve
sea salt and freshly ground black pepper

Steamed scallops with pork and pineapple rice

Ken Hom

The pork and pineapple rice on its own makes a quick and easy dinner. Combined with the fresh scallops, you have something truly special. Ken shows how to steam the scallops using hot wet vapours: a Chinese cooking technique that brings out the scallops' succulent texture and briny seafood taste without overcooking them. These dishes would also be very good with Ken's stir-fried corn and chilli (page 174).

Cook the rice according to packet instructions, then allow it to cool thoroughly by spreading it on a baking sheet. When it is cool, refrigerate. When the rice is cold, proceed with the rest of the recipe.

Heat a wok over a high heat until it is hot. Add the oil and when it is slightly smoking, add the pork and stir-fry for 2 minutes. Then add the soy sauce, salt, pepper, ginger and spring onions and continue to stir-fry for 2 minutes.

Add the rice, mix well and continue to stir-fry the mixture for another 5 minutes until the rice is heated through. Finally, add the pineapple pieces and continue to stir-fry for another 3 minutes or until the pineapple is heated through.

Meanwhile, put the scallops on a heatproof plate. Next, set up a steamer or put a rack into a deep pan and fill it with 5cm water. Bring the water to the boil over a high heat. Put the scallops on the plate into the steamer or onto the rack. Turn the heat to low and cover the pan tightly, then steam gently for 5 minutes.

Combine all the remaining ingredients except the oil and coriander sprigs in a heatproof bowl. Heat a large frying-pan over a high heat, add the oil and when it is smoking, pour this hot oil over the sauce ingredients.

Remove the scallops from the steamer and place onto a serving plate, then give the sauce several good stirs before pouring over the scallops. Garnish with the fresh coriander and serve at once with the pineapple rice.

Tip: Leftover peeled fresh root ginger can be stored in a glass jar, covered in rice wine or sherry, and sealed. It will keep for several months, is ready to use when needed and has the added benefit of producing a flavoured wine that can be used in cooking.

Serves 4

for the pork and pineapple rice
long-grain rice measured to the 400ml level in a measuring jug (or cold, leftover rice)
2 tbsp groundnut or peanut oil
225g minced pork
2 tbsp soy sauce
2 tbsp fresh ginger, finely chopped
3 tbsp spring onions, finely chopped
1 small pineapple, about 225g, peeled, cored, cut into 1cm dice
sea salt and freshly ground black pepper

for the steamed scallops
450g fresh scallops
1 tbsp fresh ginger, finely chopped
1 tbsp Shaoxing rice wine or dry sherry
2 tbsp soy sauce
1 large red mild chilli, de-seeded, chopped
3 tbsp spring onions, finely shredded
3 tbsp groundnut or vegetable oil
4 sprigs coriander, chopped

Indo-Chinese stir-fried chicken with dried chillies

Vivek Singh

The use of Indian spices alongside soy sauce is the result of a sizeable Chinese population that has lived in India for centuries. You can serve this as a starter or as a main and it also works served as nibbles on skewers; they make a great accompaniment to cocktails.

Mix together all the ingredients for the marinade, then rub them all over the chicken thighs, cover and set aside in the fridge to marinate for 30 minutes.

Heat enough oil for deep-frying in a deep-fat fryer or a deep, heavy-based pan to 190°C (or until a cube of white bread, when dropped in, turns light golden brown in about 1 minute). Add the chicken pieces and deep-fry for about 5 minutes, until they are crisp, golden-brown and just cooked through. Drain on kitchen paper and set aside.

For the stir-fry, heat the oil in a heavy pan to smoking point. Add the dried red chillies and move them around quickly. As they darken, add the cumin seeds and garlic and stir quickly. As soon as the garlic starts to change colour, add the onions and the red or green pepper and stir-fry until softened – about 2 minutes. Then add the fried chicken, salt, sugar, chilli powder and cumin and continue stir-frying on a high heat for 1–2 minutes. Finally, add the soy sauce and chicken stock cube and mix well.

When all the vegetables are softened and the spices well combined, add the cornflour paste and stir quickly to mix evenly. This gives the dish an attractive glaze and also thickens the sauce. Squeeze in the lemon juice, add the chopped wild garlic or spring onion and stir to mix.

Serve immediately with steamed rice or noodles if serving as a main, or with a simple salad of watercress as a starter.

Tip: Never let the heat in the pan reduce. Your burner should be on high throughout and you should add an ingredient to the pan only when you are sure it is hot enough.

Serves 4

700g boneless skinless chicken thighs, cut in 3–4 pieces each
oil, for deep-frying

for the marinade
3 garlic cloves, chopped
4 tbsp cornflour
1 egg, lightly beaten
1 tbsp light soy sauce
1 tbsp dark soy sauce
1 tbsp rice vinegar
½ chicken stock cube, crumbled
½ tsp salt

for the stir-fry
3 tbsp vegetable oil
2 dried red chillies, broken into pieces
1 tsp whole cumin seeds
3 garlic cloves, finely chopped
2 red onions, finely chopped
½ red or green pepper, cut into 2.5cm dice
1 tsp salt
1½ tsp sugar
1 tsp red chilli powder
1 tsp ground cumin
2 tsp dark soy sauce
½ chicken stock cube, crumbled
1 tbsp cornflour, mixed to a paste with a little water
½ lemon, juiced
2 tbsp chopped wild garlic (when in season) or spring onions

Bunny chow

Atul Kochhar

Bunny chow is a hugely popular South African street food — a hollowed-out half loaf of bread filled with curry. A bit like a curry sandwich, but nicer than that sounds – in fact, absolutely yummy! The traditional way is to use your fingers to rip and scoop your way through the bunny, but feel free to use a knife and fork at home.

Heat the oil in a pan and sauté the whole spices and bay leaf until the spices sizzle. Add the onion and cook for 5–7 minutes until translucent. Stir in the curry powder and sauté for 1 minute, then add the tomatoes and stir to mix. Cook on a medium heat, stirring often, until sauce-like.

Add the lamb, ginger, garlic, curry leaves and 300ml water, bring to the boil, then reduce the heat and simmer, stirring occasionally, for 40–50 minutes or until the meat is tender.

Add the potatoes, salt to taste and 200ml water. Continue simmering for about 15 minutes until the lamb and potatoes are perfectly cooked. Stir in the chopped coriander and lime juice.

To serve, spoon into the hollow bread and garnish with coriander cress.

Tip: Use day-old bread: the crust will have hardened and the 'tureen' will be less likely to collapse. To make a vegetarian bunny, substitute red and white kidney beans for the meat.

Serves 4

2 tbsp vegetable oil
½ tsp cumin seeds
½ tsp fennel seeds
2.5cm cinnamon stick
2 green cardamom pods
1 star anise
1 bay leaf
1 onion, finely chopped
2 tbsp South African curry powder
2 tomatoes, chopped
1kg boneless leg of lamb, cut into 1cm dice
1 tbsp finely chopped fresh ginger
1 tbsp finely chopped garlic
10–12 curry leaves
2 large potatoes, cut into 1cm dice
2 tbsp finely chopped coriander leaves
2 tbsp lime juice
2 loaves unsliced white bread, each cut in half across the middle and most of the crumbs removed
coriander cress or sprigs, to garnish
sea salt

Pheasant with cavolo nero and a chestnut stuffing

Bryn Williams

If you're a novice when it comes to cooking game, start with pheasant as it has a sweet, earthy flavour that isn't overpowering. Bryn says, 'Think of pheasant as a small, well-flavoured chicken and try using it instead of chicken in your favourite dishes.' This easy roast dinner cooks in a fraction of the time of a normal roast as it uses pheasant crowns, which provide the perfect portion for one.

Preheat the oven to 200°C/400°F/Gas 6.

Heat a large frying pan and add the oil. Once hot, add the crowns, seal on all sides and place in the oven for 8 minutes, or until the juices from the thickest part of the meat run clear when pierced with a skewer.

For the chestnut stuffing, heat a medium frying pan and add the oil. Once hot, add the pancetta and cook until crispy. Add the hazelnuts, breadcrumbs and thyme and cook for a couple of minutes. Grate in the chestnuts and keep warm.

Heat a large pan of boiling water and add the cavolo nero, blanch for 2 minutes, then drain. Heat a large frying pan, melt 1 tablespoon of the butter until foaming. Add the blanched cavolo nero and cook for a minute until wilted.

In a separate pan, heat the remaining butter, add the mushrooms and cook for a couple of minutes.

To serve, place the cavolo nero in the centre of each of 4 plates. Cut the breasts from the pheasant and place on top. Top with the stuffing and garnish with the mushrooms.

Serves 4

1 tbsp olive oil
4 pheasant crowns

for the chestnut stuffing
1 tbsp oil
100g pancetta, diced
50g skinned hazelnuts
50g Japanese panko
  breadcrumbs
2 sprigs thyme, leaves
  removed
100g cooked chestnuts

for the cavolo nero
1 cavolo nero, tough stalks
  removed, chopped
2 tbsp butter
400g wild mushrooms,
  cleaned

Tip: Don't be tempted to overcook game – all game, even the birds, can be served slightly pink, meaning it's more succulent and juicy.

Cannellini beans with spare ribs
Gennaro Contaldo

Need a little comforting at this time of year? What could be better than meltingly tender pork, a rich tomato sauce and beans, mopped up with some garlicky bruschetta. Sometimes the simplest dishes are the best!

Drain the beans, then put them in a large saucepan with about 1.8 litres water or enough to cover. Half-cover with a lid and bring to the boil, then reduce the heat to medium and simmer for 50 minutes, until tender.

Meanwhile, heat the extra virgin olive oil in a large, shallow pan. Add the ribs, bay leaves, rosemary, sage, salt and pepper and seal the ribs over a medium-high heat for 1–2 minutes on each side. Remove them and set aside.

Reduce the heat to medium, add the onion and garlic to the pan and sweat for a couple of minutes. Add the tomato passata, 500ml water and some salt and simmer for 5 minutes. Return the ribs to the pan and cook, covered, on a low heat for about 1½ hours, until the meat begins to become detached from the bone. Remove the ribs again and keep warm.

Drain the cooked beans and add to the tomato sauce, then simmer gently for 5 minutes.

Meanwhile, grill the bread, then rub each slice lightly with a cut clove of garlic and drizzle with a little of the oil.

Remove the beans from the heat and serve with the spare ribs. Garnish with parsley and chilli and serve with bruschetta.

Tip: The spare ribs are perfect like this or try them with rice, mashed potato or a bowl of soft polenta for a more substantial dinner.

Serves 4–6

200g dried cannellini beans, soaked in cold water for at least 12 hours
5 tbsp extra virgin olive oil
800g pork spare ribs, chopped into 7.5cm pieces
4 bay leaves
1 sprig rosemary, leaves only
6 fresh sage leaves
1 onion, finely chopped
1 garlic clove, finely chopped
500g tomato passata
sea salt and freshly ground black pepper

for the bruschetta
few slices ciabatta bread or good-quality sourdough
few garlic cloves, peeled
extra virgin olive oil, to drizzle

to serve
small handful flat-leaf parsley, finely chopped
1 red chilli, de-seeded and finely diced

Lamb with torn bread and apricot stuffing with chicory and onion

Bill Granger

Bill loves roast lamb – it's a dish that is as popular in Sydney as it is in London – and this is a tantalising way to cook it, stuffed with pistachio and apricots and roasted with cumin and strips of torn bread infused with the lamb juices.

For the lamb, heat the butter in a large frying pan over a medium heat. Add the onion and cook, stirring occasionally, for 6–8 minutes, or until softened. Add the crushed garlic and half of the cumin seeds and cook for another minute. Tip the mixture into a large bowl and add the torn bread, chilli flakes, dried apricots and pistachio nuts and season well with sea salt and freshly ground black pepper. Set aside until needed.

Preheat the oven to 190°C/375°F/Gas 5.

Mix the olive oil with the remaining cumin seeds and brush this mixture over the entire surface of the lamb. Place the lamb in a large roasting tin and cook for 1 hour 20 minutes in total. However, 15 minutes before the end of cooking, place the stuffing mixture in the pan around the lamb and return it to the oven.

Meanwhile, for the caramelised chicory, place the chicory and onions in a baking dish and sprinkle with the sugar and chilli flakes. Drizzle with the oil and vinegar and season to taste with sea salt and freshly ground black pepper. Place in the oven and cook for 35–45 minutes, or until golden-brown and caramelised.

Once the lamb is cooked, cover loosely with foil and leave to rest for 10–15 minutes before carving.

Serve the lamb in slices with the caramelised chicory and stuffing alongside.

Tip: White chicory, otherwise known as endive or witloof, has a distinctive cigar-shaped head. It is a forced crop – meaning it's grown in the dark to stop it turning green, but there is also a red version now. Endive is gorgeous raw, however cooking changes its character, making it endlessly versatile. Bill's bitter-sweet caramelised version, with baked onions, makes a great side for many dishes.

Serves 4–6

for the lamb
60g butter
1 onion, chopped
1 garlic clove, peeled, crushed
2 tsp cumin seeds
200g sourdough bread, torn into bite-size pieces
1 tsp dried chilli flakes
150g dried apricots, roughly chopped
50g pistachio nuts, roughly chopped
1 tbsp olive oil, for brushing
2kg lamb leg, bone in
sea salt and freshly ground black pepper

for the caramelised chicory and onion
4 white or red chicory heads, halved lengthways
3 red onions, cut into wedges
3 tbsp soft brown sugar
½ tbsp dried chilli flakes
2 tbsp olive oil
2 tbsp cider vinegar
sea salt and freshly ground black pepper

My family ragu

Gennaro Contaldo

Gennaro says, 'This has to be my favourite dish, as it is so reminiscent of my childhood. Historically, meat ragu was slow-cooked in terracotta pots for up to 12 hours, which may seem absurd, but believe me, the taste is amazing!'

Season the meat well. Heat the olive oil in a large heavy-based pan, then add the meat and brown evenly all over. Add the onion, carrot and bay leaves and fry gently over a medium heat until the onion has softened slightly.

Add 150ml of the red wine and bubble away to evaporate slightly. Put the remaining wine in a glass and stir in the tomato purée until smooth, then add to the pan along with the tinned tomatoes and 3 tins of water. Stir well and bring to the boil.

Add the basil, reduce the heat to low, cover with a lid and cook for 2–3 hours, checking and stirring from time to time. An hour before the sauce is ready, check the consistency. If the sauce is too runny, then simmer with the lid removed for the remaining hour, stirring occasionally.

Cook the tagliatelle in boiling salted water according to the packet instructions until al dente, then drain.

Remove the ragu from the heat, season to taste and flake all the meat from the pork ribs. Shred the beef, discarding the bones and bay leaves. Serve tossed through the tagliatelle with plenty of grated Parmesan.

Tip: The wine you should cook with is the wine you are drinking: do not use cooking wine or, as Gennaro calls it, 'coloured water'!

Serves 8

500g beef topside
   (or brisket), cut into
   individual ribs
500g pork spare ribs
200g pork sausages, casings
   removed
5 tbsp olive oil
1 small onion, finely chopped
1 small carrot, finely chopped
3 bay leaves
250ml rich Italian red wine
2 tbsp tomato purée
3 x 400g tins chopped plum
   tomatoes
handful basil leaves, torn
700g tagliatelle
30g Parmesan, finely grated
sea salt and freshly ground
   black pepper

Baked pork chops with pears and Roquefort butter

Diana Henry

More than anything, you need recipes that are truly useful, and these chops are the perfect bung-it-in-the-oven midweek supper grub. The beauty of Diana's food is in throwing together ingredients that get along: pears and pork, creamy blue cheese with crunchy toasted walnuts and bitter-sweet chicory leaves.

For the Roquefort butter, place the butter and Roquefort into a bowl and mash together with a wooden spoon. Chill in the freezer for 10 minutes, then spoon onto a sheet of cling film and roll up into a sausage shape, twisting up the ends to seal. Place in the fridge to chill for 1 hour, or until firm.

Preheat the oven to 200°C/400°F/Gas 6.

For the pork chops, place the potato slices in a roasting tin with the thyme and drizzle over half the olive oil. Season well with salt and freshly ground black pepper. Toss well to coat, then place the onions, pears (cut-side down) and pork chops on top.

Drizzle over the remaining oil, season again with salt and freshly ground black pepper, then toss lightly to coat in the oil.

Place in the oven to cook for 15 minutes, or until the pork is lightly golden. Reduce the oven heat to 190°C/375°F/Gas 5, then remove the tin from the oven.

Turn the chops over and turn over the pears so that they are cut-side up. Sprinkle the pears with the brown sugar, then return the tin to the oven. Roast for another 30–40 minutes, or until the pork is golden-brown and cooked through, the pears caramelised and the potatoes tender.

For the salad, place the watercress, chicory and walnuts into a bowl. In a smaller bowl, whisk together the vinegar, cassis and oil, then season with salt and freshly ground black pepper. Drizzle the dressing over the salad, then toss well to coat.

To serve, spoon the pork chops, potatoes and pears onto 4 plates and place the salad alongside. Slice a knob of Roquefort butter and place over the top of each pork chop to melt.

Serves 4

for the Roquefort butter
75g butter, at room temperature
50g Roquefort, crumbled

for the pork chops
500g waxy potatoes, cut into 2mm thick slices
8 sprigs thyme
6 tbsp olive oil
2 red onions, peeled, cut into 8 wedges each
6 small Conference pears, halved, cored
4 x 225g bone-in pork chops
50g soft dark brown sugar
sea salt and freshly ground black pepper

for the chicory, walnut and watercress salad
110g watercress, picked
110g chicory, leaves separated
110g shelled walnuts, toasted
1½ tbsp red wine vinegar
½ tsp crème de cassis or honey
4 tbsp walnut oil
sea salt and freshly ground black pepper

Braised beef with ginger, cabbage and Tom's signature glazed carrots

Tom Kerridge

Tom marinates the beef for up to 48 hours to tenderise the meat, before braising in red wine, ginger and stock until gorgeously gelatinous. A sprinkling of toasted caraway seeds adds depth of flavour and cuts through the richness of the dish. But it is Tom's signature glazed carrots that are the real stars here – sweet and tender, with a festive touch from the star anise, they take the humble carrot to a whole new level.

Place the beef shin pieces into a large bowl with the red wine, cover and leave to marinate in the fridge for 24–48 hours. Strain the shins through a sieve, reserving the wine, then pat the shins dry.

Preheat the oven to 170°C/325°F/Gas 3.

Bring the red wine to the boil in a saucepan and skim off the scum that comes to the top. Heat a large heavy-based pan until medium hot, add a little vegetable oil and the onion, carrot, celery and ginger and cook until browned.

In a separate frying pan, fry the shins in a little oil until browned very well. Drain them in a colander to get rid of any excess cooking fat. Place the shins on top of the vegetables in the pan, cover with the skimmed red wine and veal stock. Add the bay leaves, clove, white peppercorns, thyme and salt. Bring to a simmer, cover with a lid, then place in the oven to braise for 2½ hours.

When cooked, remove from the oven and leave the shins to cool down in the stock. When cool, remove the shins from the stock and pass the stock through a fine metal sieve into a saucepan and skim off any fat. Place the pan of liquid back on to the heat and cook over a medium heat until reduced to half the volume, then pass through a fine sieve again. To reheat the shins, warm them through in a covering of shin stock.

For the carrots, place all the ingredients in a saucepan with 200ml water and cook over a medium heat until the carrots are soft. Turn the heat up and cook over a high heat until the liquid glazes the carrots.

For the cabbage, heat a frying pan until medium hot, add the butter and cabbage, cover and cook until just tender. Stir in the caraway seeds and season.

To serve, pile the cabbage onto the plates, place the carrots alongside and then finish with the beef shins and sauce.

Serves 6

for the braised beef
6 x 225g pieces of beef shin
750ml red wine
vegetable oil
200g onions, roughly chopped
150g carrots, roughly chopped
150g celery sticks, roughly chopped
75g fresh ginger, grated with skin on
1.5 litres veal or beef stock
5 bay leaves
1 clove
1 tbsp white peppercorns
1 bunch thyme
3 tsp sea salt

for the glazed carrots
6 carrots, halved lengthways
125g butter
75g sugar
1½ tsp salt
4 star anise, wrapped in muslin cloth

for the cabbage
knob of butter
1 Savoy cabbage, cut into large strips
2 tbsp caraway seeds, toasted
sea salt and freshly ground black pepper

Menu: Chinese New Year

The New Year festivities extend over a period of two weeks, so this menu is all about variety and sharing. Pick a few dishes over several nights, or get family and friends together to help prepare one big, traditional feast. The prawn toast, dim sum and pork belly are quick and easy crowd-pleasers. Ken's pigeon takes more time and patience, but it isn't difficult to make and much of the work can be done in advance. Sip on pot after pot of jasmine tea and end the night with a bowl of tangerines and oranges, which symbolise luck and wealth in the year to come.

Starters

Sesame prawn toast by Annabel Langbein (page 171)

Prawn dim sum by James Martin (page 171)

———————

Main

Quick pickled cucumber or stir-fried corn and chilli (page 174) with twice-cooked pork by Ching-He Huang (page 175)

———————

Dessert

Tangerines and oranges and a pot of jasmine tea

———————

Sesame prawn toast

Annabel Langbein

You can make the topping and cut up the bread the day before. Keep them in separate airtight containers in the fridge until you're ready to assemble and cook them at the last minute.

Preheat the oven to 180°C/350°F/Gas 4. Line a baking tray with non-stick baking paper for easy clean-up.

Cut the bread slices into quarters. Mix the prawn meat with the mayonnaise, sesame oil and salt and pepper. Spread on the bread and sprinkle with sesame seeds.

Place on the prepared baking tray and bake for about 15–20 minutes until the toast is golden and crispy. Garnish with chives, if using. Best enjoyed hot from the oven.

Serves 4–6

6 slices white toast bread, crusts removed
250g raw prawn meat, finely chopped
60g speedy mayonnaise (page 216)
1 tsp sesame oil
1 tbsp sesame seeds
chopped chives (optional)
sea salt and freshly ground black pepper

Prawn dim sum

James Martin

Dim sum – or 'delicacies that touch the heart' – are easy to make with shop-bought dumpling wrappers and a couple of bamboo steamers. Plan ahead and you can freeze these in an airtight container, then cook from frozen.

For the dips, place the soy sauce, sesame oil and 1 of the chopped red chillies into a clean bowl and whisk together.

Meanwhile, place the rice vinegar, sugar and the remaining chopped red chilli into a pan and heat until the sugar dissolves. Remove from the heat and allow to cool, then pour into a clean bowl.

For the prawn dim sum, place the prawns into a small food processor and blend to a purée. Transfer to a bowl, add all the other ingredients, except the dim sum wrappers, and mix thoroughly.

Place the wrappers on a clean work surface and put a small spoonful of prawn mixture in the centre of each wrapper. Fold the wrappers over the prawn mixture to create a semi-circle. Press the edges of the wrapper together with damp fingers to seal the wrapper parcels and crimp the edges using a fork.

Place the parcels in a bamboo steamer over a pan of simmering water and cover. Steam for 4–5 minutes or until the prawn mixture is completely cooked through. Serve immediately alongside the dips.

Makes 16 dumplings

for the dips
3 tbsp soy sauce
1 tbsp sesame oil
2 red chillies, finely chopped
3 tbsp rice vinegar
1 tbsp sugar

for the prawn dim sum
250g raw king prawns, shelled, de-veined
50g bamboo shoots, finely sliced
1 tbsp sesame oil
1 tbsp Shaoxing rice wine or dry sherry
¼ tsp ground white pepper
1 tsp caster sugar
1 tsp salt
16 dumpling pastry wrappers (available from Asian supermarkets or www. theasiancookshop.co.uk)

Winter

Stir-fried corn and chilli

Ken Hom

This is a super-easy side dish that goes with everything. A great accompaniment for this Chinese New Year feast or for Ken's steamed scallops with pork and pineapple rice (page 152).

If the corn is fresh, cut the kernels off the cob. Blanch frozen corn for 5 seconds in boiling water and drain.

Heat a wok or large sauté pan until it is hot. Add the oil, salt, corn and chillies and stir-fry for 1 minute. Put in the pepper, sugar and stock and continue to cook for 3 minutes. Set aside until ready to serve.

Serves 4

275g fresh or frozen sweetcorn (about 2 cobs)
1½ tbsp groundnut or vegetable oil
2 large red chillies, de-seeded, finely chopped
1 tsp sugar
50ml vegetable or chicken stock (pages 212 or 214)
sea salt and freshly ground white pepper

Quick pickled cucumber

Ching-He Huang

Paired with garlic, chilli and rice vinegar, Ching's pickled cucumbers add a salty-sour zing to plain rice and stir-fried vegetables. This is a quick pickling technique and the pickle should be eaten within a few days while the cucumbers retain their crunch and freshness.

Slice the cucumbers in half lengthways and de-seed. Cut each half into long wedge shapes and then slice into 1cm pieces.

Combine the garlic, sugar, vinegar, chilli bean paste, chilli oil and sesame oil in a bowl. Add the cucumbers and leave to marinate in the fridge for 20 minutes.

Divide the mixture into small bowls, garnish with the fresh chilli and serve or decant into sterilised glass jars and refrigerate for up to 1 week.

Serves 2–4

4 small cucumbers
1 garlic clove, peeled, crushed
2 pinches caster sugar
1 tbsp Chinese rice vinegar (or cider vinegar)
1 tsp chilli bean paste
1 tsp chilli oil
1 tbsp toasted sesame oil
1 red chilli, de-seeded, cut into strips, to garnish

Twice-cooked pork

Ching-He Huang

Pork belly poached then fried with lots of Chinese flavourings. The best cuts to use for this classic Sichuan dish are pork belly, shoulder or collar. In Chinese, these are known as wu hua rou or the five layers of heaven – skin, fat, meat, fat, meat. The crisp pork skin literally melts in your mouth and the rich flavours of the pork belly taste absolutely delicious combined with jasmine rice.

For the pork, pour 700ml water into a large pan, add the pork and bring to the boil, then boil for 30 minutes. Drain and leave to cool.

Put the meat in the fridge for about 1 hour, to firm up, then cut into very thin slices, about 5mm thick.

Heat a wok over a high heat and add the groundnut oil, then the pork. As the pork starts to brown, add the rice wine (or sherry) and cook until the pork is browned and the skin is slightly crisp.

Add the chilli bean paste, yellow bean sauce and fermented black beans and stir-fry for 1 minute. Add the spring onion (or leek), if using, and stir-fry for less than 1 minute until well mixed. Add both soy sauces and the sugar and season, to taste.

To serve, place a spoonful of rice onto each plate and spoon the pork over the top, then arrange the pickles alongside.

Serves 4

for the pork
300g fatty pork belly, skin on
2 tbsp groundnut oil
1 tbsp Shaoxing rice wine or
   dry sherry
1 tbsp chilli bean paste
1 tbsp yellow bean sauce
1 tbsp fermented black
   beans, rinsed, crushed
1 spring onion (or baby leek),
   sliced on the diagonal into
   julienne strips (optional)
1 tsp dark soy sauce
1 tsp light soy sauce
pinch of sugar
sea salt and freshly ground
   white pepper

to serve
300g jasmine rice, steamed
quick pickled cucumber
   (page 174)

Desserts

Anyone who orders a pudding in a restaurant is making a clear statement of intent. A pudding, the finale to a meal, is a little wickedness – it is surplus to requirements. It is a treat, a moment of joy and offers the potential to nourish the soul in a truly unique way. It is so important to prepare and cook desserts with this in mind. For the most part we are looking for velvety smooth creams, buttery biscuit-based crunch or a combination of the two. Whilst soft and sensuous alone is sometimes just the ticket, it is often the contrast between a firm-textured component and an oozing centre that works so incredibly well.

To achieve these textures, or mouthfeel as it is sometimes called, it is key to follow recipes carefully. The world of savoury cooking is mostly about proceeding with loose reins and using plenty of judgement. The world of dessert making, or pastry as it is professionally known, is not so much about pan-spanking flair as accurate measurement and going about things in a logical and professional manner. Read the recipe from start to finish to get an overall picture of what lies ahead. Ensure you have every piece of equipment specified to hand, spotlessly clean. Clear the decks. If making pastry, chill the bowls to be used. If needed, create space in the fridge for chilling any components that require it. In a nutshell, think ahead and prepare yourself and your kitchen for what is to come.

Being able to produce a dessert with its inherent deliciousness intact relies on one's ability to understand exactly what makes it work so well in the first place. It is the warm, soft homeliness of Wolfgang Puck's Kaiserschmarren that is brought to life with a dusting of icing sugar and some strawberry compote. It is the fine pastry, rich crème pâtissière and quality fruit that will make Richard Bertinet's tartlets the sensations they deserve to be. The success of Angela Hartnett's mini pavlovas lies in the exact whipping of the cream – so that it remains a dolloping and voluptuous wonder, not a stiffly whipped inert mass.

For those of us lucky enough to be born with a sweet tooth, the making of desserts provides us with an opportunity to get lost in a world of cooking that can deliver fulfilment and pleasure in equal measure. Enjoy!

Phil Howard

Little fudge biscuits

Martin Morales

These little biscuits might look dainty, but the flavours of the rich chocolate fudge and the sharp-tasting, fruity physalis sauce really pack a punch. You can serve them as a dessert in individual portions, but they are delicate enough to work well as petits fours.

Preheat the oven to 160°C/325°F/Gas 3.

To make the coulis, put the physalis in a saucepan with 50ml water. Add the caster sugar and simmer for about 15 minutes or until it has reduced and looks sticky and syrupy. Keep an eye on it as you don't want it to caramelise or burn. Add the lime juice and then either blitz in a food processor or blender or strain through a sieve, making a thick, jammy sauce. Set aside.

Now, make the biscuits. Using a hand mixer, whip the egg yolks in a bowl until they are airy and lighter in colour. You should be able to form a thick ribbon when you trail your whisk through them. Gradually add in the pisco and the butter while mixing, and then add the flour, baking powder and salt. Add a sprinkling of water, if needed. Knead the dough until it is smooth.

Roll out the dough to 1–2mm thick on a lightly floured work surface. Using a 5cm cutter, cut into rounds and put on a baking tray lined with non-stick baking paper. Prick the rounds all over with a fork to prevent them puffing. Bake in the oven for 10 minutes or until a light golden brown and then remove and leave to cool.

To make the fudge, gently heat the evaporated milk and sugar in a saucepan and warm through until the sugar has dissolved. Remove from the heat, leave to cool for a couple of minutes and then stir in the chocolate and butter. Continue to stir until completely melted and you have a very thick, smooth fudge. Do not refrigerate as this will firm up the fudge too much and it will be hard to spread.

To serve, create stacks of the biscuits by sandwiching 3 together with some fudge. Place 2 stacks on a plate, dust with icing sugar and spoon some physalis coulis alongside. Decorate with a few whole physalis if you wish.

Tip: You can make the coulis ahead of time: it will keep for about a month if stored in the fridge.

Makes about 30 biscuits

for the physalis coulis
100g physalis, husks removed
50g caster sugar
½ lime, juiced

for the biscuits
3 egg yolks
2 tsp pisco brandy (or white tequila)
15g butter, softened
100g plain flour, plus extra for dusting
1 tsp baking powder
pinch salt

for the fudge
100ml evaporated milk
25g caster sugar
100g dark chocolate, minimum 70 per cent cocoa solids, broken into pieces
10g butter

to serve
icing sugar
few whole physalis (optional)

Fruity biscotti

James Martin

Biscotti are hard, Italian-style cookies that are baked twice – first in loaves, then cut into oblongs – to give them their crunchy texture and amazingly long shelf life. (A staple of the Roman legions, Pliny the Elder once boasted that they would be edible for centuries!) They are perfect for dunking into a cup of tea or strong coffee, but for true Italian style, an ice-cold limoncello (page 209), served in frozen shot glasses, is hard to beat.

Preheat the oven to 180°C/350°F/Gas 4 and line a baking tray with non-stick baking paper.

Mix the flour, sugar and baking powder together in a large bowl. Add half the beaten eggs and mix well, then add half of what's left and mix again. Now add the last quarter a little bit at a time until the dough takes shape, but isn't too wet (you may not need to use all the eggs).

Add the dried fruit and lemon zest and mix well. Divide the dough in half and each half into a sausage shape and place on the baking tray, leaving at least a 6cm gap between them. Lightly flatten the 'sausages', then bake for 20–30 minutes until golden brown. Remove from the oven and leave for 10 minutes to cool and firm up.

Turn the oven down to 150°C/300°F/Gas 2. Once cooled, move the cooked biscotti dough onto a chopping board. Using a serrated knife, cut the biscotti on an angle into 5mm slices. Lay the slices on the baking tray. Return to the oven and cook for 8 minutes, then turn the slices over and cook for a further 10–15 minutes or until pale golden brown. Remove from the oven and cool the biscotti on wire racks.

Serves 4

250g plain flour
250g caster sugar
1½ tsp baking powder
2 large eggs, lightly beaten
90g sultanas
90g raisins
90g dried sour cherries
110g dried apricots, roughly
    chopped
1 unwaxed lemon, finely
    grated zest only

Tip: James's fruity biscotti are great, make-ahead Christmas gifts and they hold up well in the post too. If you're in a generous mood, make one batch for yourself and another for family and friends.

The emperor's trifle (Kaiserschmarren)
Wolfgang Puck

This is an Austrian classic. Wolfgang's version, flavoured with rum and raisins and dusted with sugar, comes out as light and delicate as a soufflé, and tastes like heaven. Perfect for a dinner party or, if you're feeling decadent, eat it for breakfast instead!

For the strawberry compote, set aside 350g of the strawberries and 60g of the sugar. In a heavy saucepan, combine the remaining strawberries, 125ml water, 115g of the sugar, the orange juice, star anise and Grand Marnier. Bring to a boil over a medium heat, stirring occasionally to prevent scorching. Reduce the heat and simmer for 10 minutes.

Remove the strawberries from the heat, cover with cling film and allow to infuse for 10 minutes. Discard the star anise, then pour the mixture into a blender and blitz to a fine purée. Pass the sauce through a very fine sieve and reserve in a pan ready to use, or refrigerate if not using right away.

Preheat the oven to 210°C/425°F/Gas 7. For the Kaiserschmarren, generously butter 2 ovenproof dishes, 22cm in diameter. Dust each pan with sugar and tap out any excess.

In a medium bowl using a hand mixer, beat the egg yolks with 25g of the caster sugar until the mixture is light and lemony yellow. Beat in the fromage blanc and mix until well combined. Beat in the crème fraîche and the rum, scrape down the bowl and beaters, then beat in the flour and raisins and set aside.

In another very clean bowl, use a hand mixer or stand mixer to whisk the egg whites on medium-low speed until they foam, then add the cream of tartar. Turn the speed up to medium and continue to beat while slowly pouring in the remaining 150g sugar. Whisk until medium stiff peaks form when the whisk is removed.

Whisk half the egg whites into the crème fraîche base, then gently fold in the remaining egg whites. Divide the batter equally between the 2 sugared pans.

Serves 4

for the strawberry compote
950g strawberries, hulled and
    quartered
175g caster sugar
175ml orange juice
1 star anise, lightly toasted
1 tbsp Grand Marnier or other
    orange liqueur

for the Kaiserschmarren
50g butter, softened, to
    butter the pans
175g caster sugar, plus extra
    for dusting the pans
4 large egg yolks and
    8 large egg whites,
    at room temperature
110g fromage blanc (or quark
    or crème fraîche)
175g crème fraîche
75ml dark rum
75g plain flour
60g golden raisins, soaked in
    4 tbsp white wine
½ tsp cream of tartar
60g icing sugar, for dusting

Bake in the middle of the oven for 15 minutes. Turn the pans if browning unevenly and bake for another 5–8 minutes, until puffed and brown. The centre should be set and slightly firm.

Meanwhile, in a large saucepan, bring the strawberry compote to a boil over a high heat. Add the reserved 60g of sugar and stir until the sugar has dissolved. Reduce for 1 minute. Add the reserved 350g of cut strawberries and toss to coat.

To serve, divide the strawberry compote among the serving plates. When the Kaiserschmarren are done, remove from the oven and, using a serving spoon, divide each one into 2 portions. Dust with icing sugar and serve immediately.

Tip: Strawberries or raspberries make a classic summer compote, or you can ring the changes with an apple or damson compote, preserved plums or some luscious fresh berries on the side.

Orange and almond cake

James Martin

Made with ground almonds and whole oranges – simmered until very tender, then roughly chopped – this classic Spanish cake is wonderfully light and moist with the zingiest, sunniest orange sauce that James can dream up.

For the orange cake, simmer the 2 whole oranges in a saucepan of simmering water for 45–60 minutes, or until very soft. Remove the pan from the heat and leave the oranges to cool in the water.

Preheat the oven to 180°C/350°F/Gas 4. Grease the cake tin with butter.

Drain the oranges and roughly chop, discarding the pips. In a food processor, blend 450g of the chopped orange to a purée. Add the sugar, eggs and ground almonds and blend until smooth. Spoon the mixture into the cake tin.

Bake in the oven for 25 minutes, then cover loosely with foil and bake for a further 25–35 minutes, or until cooked through (a skewer inserted in the middle should come out clean). Remove from the oven and set aside to cool.

For the caramel and orange sauce, heat a frying pan until hot, add the butter, orange zest and juice and the caster sugar. Add the orange liqueur and brandy and flambé by slowly tilting the pan towards the flame or lighting with a match. Do this carefully. Let the flames flare up, then die down. Cook for a few minutes until just thickened and bubbling, then add the orange segments and remove the pan from the heat.

To serve, put a slice of cake on each plate and pour the sauce over the cake and around the plate. Serve immediately with a scoop of ice cream, if you like.

Serves 8

You'll need a 23cm springform cake tin

for the cake
2 oranges, scrubbed
butter, for greasing
225g caster sugar
6 medium eggs
250g ground almonds

for the caramel and orange sauce
50g butter
1 orange, zest and juice
2 oranges, juice only
3 tbsp caster sugar
2 tbsp orange liqueur
2 tbsp brandy
1 orange, segmented

to serve
vanilla ice cream (optional)

Fruit tartlets

Richard Bertinet

Richard's exquisite little tarts are filled with a classic, vanilla-infused crème pâtissière and topped with summer berries. You can make them in other sizes; you might prefer just one big tart, which can be cut into slices. If you're making these for a dinner party, you can blind bake the pastry cases in batches a few days in advance – they keep well, stored in an airtight container.

Lightly grease and flour the tins.

Skim a fine film of flour over your work surface, roll out the pastry 2–3mm thick and use to line the tins. Line with non-stick baking paper and ceramic beans. Place in the fridge to rest for at least 30 minutes.

Preheat the oven to 190°C/375°F/Gas 5.

Remove the tins from the fridge, place on a baking tray and bake for 15 minutes. Lift out the paper and beans, brush the pastry with the beaten egg, then bake for another 8 minutes. Set aside.

To make the filling, place the milk, vanilla seeds and pod into a large saucepan and warm though. Place the egg yolks, sugar and flour in a large glass bowl and whisk until the colour changes. Gradually add the warm milk and vanilla and whisk and return to the pan. Cook on a low heat until it thickens, pour into a clean bowl and cover with a greaseproof lid to stop a skin forming.

If you would like to flavour the crème with kirsch, add it to the crème once it is cold.

To make up the tartlets, either pipe or spoon the crème pâtissière into the pastry cases and top with the fresh fruit. Put the apricot jam and 1 tablespoon water in a small saucepan and warm it through, so it loosens up and becomes more liquid. Lightly brush the fruit to glaze.

To serve, place the tarts on a cake stand, dust with icing sugar and garnish with chopped pistachio nuts.

Tip: If you're short of time, forgo making your own pastry and buy ready-made pastry cases (available from most supermarkets).

Makes 6

You'll need six 8 x 2cm loose-bottomed tartlet tins

½ x quantity sweet pastry (page 224)
1 egg, beaten with a pinch of salt, for sealing the pastry

for the crème pâtissière
250ml whole milk
1 vanilla pod, seeds removed and pod retained
3 egg yolks
60g caster sugar
25g plain flour
2 tbsp kirsch (optional)

for the toppings
200g strawberries, hulled and quartered
50g redcurrants
50g raspberries
50g blackberries

to serve
100g clear apricot jam
25g icing sugar
50g pistachios, roughly chopped

Desserts

Mini pavlovas with strawberry sauce and vanilla cream

Angela Hartnett

Summer on a plate! Make the meringues in advance and let them cool slowly for the perfect gooey, airy crunch. Served with a dollop of strawberry sauce and vanilla cream and a scattering of fresh raspberries, Angela's classic confections are as easy as they are impressive.

Preheat the oven to 125°C/250°F/Gas ½. Line a baking tray with non-stick baking paper.

For the mini pavlovas, place the egg whites in the bowl of a large food processor or stand mixer with a whisk attachment (make sure the bowl is scrupulously clean, without a speck of grease). Whisk until soft peaks form when the whisk is removed. Gradually whisk in the sugar until the egg whites are firm. Fold in the cornflour and vinegar.

Spoon the meringue into small nest shapes on the lined baking tray and place in the oven for 10 minutes. Reduce the heat to 100°C/200°F/Gas ¼ and cook for an hour. Leave in the oven overnight to cool completely.

For the strawberry sauce and vanilla cream, place the cream and vanilla seeds in a large bowl and whisk until soft peaks form when the whisk is removed. Set aside. Place the strawberries into a food processor with the icing sugar and lemon juice. Blend to a purée and then pass through a fine sieve into a bowl.

To serve, place the meringue nests on to serving plates and spoon the vanilla cream on top, then add the strawberries and raspberries and drizzle with the sauce. Garnish with mint leaves and a dusting of icing sugar.

Serves 8

for the pavlovas
6 medium egg whites
300g caster sugar
1 tsp cornflour
1 tsp white wine vinegar

for the strawberry sauce and vanilla cream
400ml double cream
1 vanilla pod, seeds removed
500g strawberries, hulled
1–2 tbsp icing sugar
1 lemon, juiced

to serve
200g strawberries, hulled and quartered
200g raspberries
2 sprigs mint, leaves picked
2 tbsp icing sugar

Tip: Take care to separate the eggs properly (even a speck of egg yolk can ruin the whites). And don't be tempted to overbeat the egg whites. Once you have the mix whipped to glossy perfection, bake the meringues straightaway. Left to stand for too long, the egg whites will start to collapse, and make a meringue that is less impressively airy.

Sticky toffee pudding with a hot toffee sauce

James Martin

Sticky and sweet, rich and indulgent – a slab of this, drenched in hot toffee sauce, with a scoop of vanilla ice cream on the side, is guaranteed to win you friends!

Preheat the oven to 200°C/400°F/Gas 6. Butter the pudding basins really well with a third of the softened butter, then dust with the plain flour.

Place the dates and 300ml water in a saucepan and simmer for about 5 minutes.

Whisk the remaining butter and the sugar together in a large bowl using a hand mixer until light and fluffy. Gradually add the golden syrup, treacle, vanilla extract and eggs to the mixture and continue beating. Turn the beaters down to a slow speed and add the self-raising flour, a spoon at a time. Beat until all the ingredients are well combined.

Purée the hot water and date mixture in a food processor or blender and add the bicarbonate of soda. Quickly add this to the mixture in the bowl while it is still hot. Stir to combine and fill the pudding basins with the mixture. Bake in the oven for 15–20 minutes until the top is just firm to the touch.

For the sauce, place all the sauce ingredients in a pan and bring to the boil. Remove from the heat.

To serve, remove the puddings from the basins and put on a serving plate with lots of hot sauce on the top and serve with vanilla ice cream on the side.

Tip: Any dried dates are fine to use, but the fresh, fat and juicy Medjool dates have a toffee-like sweetness that works perfectly here. Look out for these in wintertime, in supermarkets or at your local greengrocer.

Serves 8

You'll need 8 x 7.5cm metal pudding basins

for the pudding
90g butter, softened
30g plain flour
200g dried stoneless dates
  (also see tip)
170g dark brown sugar
1 tbsp golden syrup
2 tbsp black treacle
½ tsp vanilla extract
2 eggs
200g self-raising flour
1 tsp bicarbonate of soda

for the sauce
200ml double cream
80g butter
80g dark brown sugar
4 tbsp black treacle
2 tbsp golden syrup

to serve
vanilla ice cream

Baked apple with spiced custard and apple granita

Sat Bains

A quintessentially English dessert, made elegant and modern with Sat's custard flavoured with locally foraged pine, is delicious served with a refreshing Bramley apple granita.

For the apple granita, juice the apples using a juicer (or alternatively use bought apple juice). Add a little sugar if it is too sour, then strain through a fine metal sieve into a freezable tub. Freeze until completely frozen.

Preheat the oven to 240°C/475°F/Gas 9.

Use a pastry brush to coat the apples in some of the butter and sprinkle over the sugar. Set aside until needed.

Place the remaining baked apple ingredients, except the mixed spice and zests, into a pan. Bring to the boil and simmer for 2 minutes. Remove from the heat and add the mixed spice and zest.

Divide the mixture into the ovenproof dishes or ramekins and top with the halved apples. Transfer to the oven and bake for 10 minutes. Reduce the oven temperature to 160°C/325°F/Gas 3 and cook for approximately 10 minutes until soft, then set aside.

For the pine custard, in a pan bring the milk, cream and pine needles up to the boil. Turn off the heat and set aside for 30 minutes to infuse. When the mix has infused, slowly bring back up to the boil and remove from the heat.

Whisk together the egg yolks and sugar in a large heatproof bowl until pale.

Gradually pour the infused milk into the egg yolk mixture, whisking constantly until the mixture has cooled down slightly, then strain through a fine metal sieve into a clean pan. Return the mixture to a very low heat and stir with a wooden spoon until the mixture coats the back of the spoon.

When ready to serve, scrape the frozen apple juice with the back of a spoon to form a granita. To serve, divide the custard into 4 bowls, then place a baked apple half on top and sprinkle over the granita. Serve at once.

Tip: If there are Douglas fir pine trees in your neighbourhood, make sure they haven't been sprayed with pesticides and pick your own needles choosing young tips, which are lighter in colour and softer than the older needles.

Serves 4

You'll need a juicer and 4 ramekins or small ovenproof dishes

for the granita
4 Bramley apples (or 125ml shop-bought apple juice)
sugar, to taste

for the baked apples
2 Bramley apples, peeled, cut in half horizontally and core removed
100g butter, softened
50g demerara sugar
110g raisins
50ml double cream
110g soft brown sugar
1 tsp mixed spice
1 lemon, zest only
1 orange, zest only

for the pine custard
250ml milk
250ml cream
50g fresh Douglas fir pine needles
200g pasteurised or fresh egg yolks
80g caster sugar

Walnut and pistachio baklava with almond and ginger ice cream

James Martin

Pretty and fragrant, James's flaky diamonds of baklava look impressive, but are surprisingly easy to make at home. The same goes for the ice cream – an addictively crunchy almond and ginger flavour, which sounds sophisticated, but is essentially a simple, flavoured cream. Both can be made a few days in advance.

Preheat the oven to 180°C/350°F/Gas 4.

For the baklava, brush a 25 x 18cm baking tray with some of the melted butter. Trim the filo pastry to fit the baking tray if necessary (scissors work better than a knife for this job). Then place one of the sheets in the tray. Brush with butter, then place another filo sheet on top and brush with butter. Repeat to use up half of the filo sheets in this way.

Meanwhile, mix the walnuts and pistachio nuts together in a bowl. Pour the nut mixture onto the buttered filo pastry stack and spread out evenly.

Brush one more sheet of filo with butter, then place it butter-side down on the layer of nuts. Brush the sheet with butter, then repeat the layering process with the remaining filo sheets, again buttering each sheet before adding the next.

Using a large sharp knife, score the top of the layered stack in a diamond pattern. Place in the oven and bake for 20–25 minutes, until golden and cooked through.

Meanwhile, place the caster sugar, 200ml water, lemon juice and ground ginger in a pan over a medium heat and bring to the boil. Boil for 5–6 minutes, until just thickened to a syrup.

When the baklava comes out of the oven, pour the warm syrup over and set aside to cool.

For the ice cream, place the cream, ginger syrup, ground ginger and honey into a freezer-safe bowl and whisk until soft peaks are formed when the whisk is removed. Add the chopped almonds and ginger and fold together gently.

Place in the freezer for 2–4 hours, or until set solid. Remove the ice cream from the freezer 10 minutes before serving.

To serve, separate the baklava diamonds and place 2 onto each plate. Top with a scoop of ice cream and serve.

Serves 4–6

for the baklava
150g butter, melted
270g filo pastry
110g walnuts, finely chopped
110g pistachio nuts, finely
    chopped
250g caster sugar
½ lemon, juiced
½ tsp ground ginger

for the ice cream
250ml double cream
50ml syrup from a jar of
    stem ginger
¼ tsp ground ginger
2 tbsp honey
50g almonds, roughly
    chopped
50g stem ginger, finely
    chopped

Greengage, nectarine and gooseberry fool

Phil Howard

Phil's light, luscious fool, spiked with almond crumble, delivers some of the great flavours of summer in splashes of orange and green. The nectarines can be poached and the gooseberry compote made up to 12 hours in advance, as long as you store them in the fridge. The almond crumble can be made then too. Finishing the fool with the whipped cream is a five-minute job that should be left as late as possible – ideally just before serving, but certainly no more than two hours in advance.

Preheat the oven to 170°C/325°F/Gas 3. Lightly grease a baking tray.

For the almond crumble, place all the dry ingredients into a stand mixer fitted with the paddle attachment. Mix briefly at medium speed, then add the butter and mix until a crumbly dough forms.

Crumble the dough onto the greased baking tray and place in the oven for 20 minutes, or until golden-brown, and then remove from the oven and set aside to cool.

For the gooseberry jelly, place the gooseberries, sugar, lemon juice and 200ml water in a bowl and set it over a pan of simmering water, making sure the water doesn't touch the base of the bowl. Cover with a lid and leave for 1 hour.

Pour the mixture through a fine sieve into a bowl, discarding the solids. Measure out 400ml of the gooseberry juice, pour into a pan and heat to near-boiling point. Remove from the heat.

Squeeze out any excess water from the softened gelatine and add the gelatine to the juice. Whisk until the gelatine dissolves. Divide the mixture into 8 round-bottomed glasses and leave it to cool. Place in the fridge to set.

For the poached nectarines, put the sugar and wine into a heavy-based pan, add 500ml water and bring to the boil, stirring until the sugar is dissolved.

Gently drop the nectarines into the poaching syrup. Bring back to the boil over a medium heat, then turn the heat down, cover and cook at a low simmer for 8–10 minutes, until the nectarines are tender when tested with a small, sharp knife.

Remove the pan from the heat and set aside to cool to room temperature. Lift the fruit out of the syrup and pull off the skins, then return the fruit to the syrup and set aside, covered, at room temperature.

Serves 8

for the almond crumble
80g plain flour
80g ground almonds
80g demerara sugar
80g caster sugar
pinch salt
80g butter, chilled, diced

for the gooseberry jelly
500g gooseberries, halved
125g caster sugar
½ lemon, juiced
2 gelatine leaves, soaked in
    cold water for 5 minutes

for the poached nectarines
250g caster sugar
150ml rosé wine
4 large, ripe nectarines,
    halved, stones removed

for the gooseberry fool
300g gooseberries, stalks
    removed, halved
75g caster sugar
½ lemon, zest and juice
300ml double cream
2 vanilla pods, seeds
    removed
50g icing sugar

to garnish
8 ripe, firm greengages,
    halved, stones removed

Desserts

For the gooseberry fool, place the gooseberries in a heavy-based pan and add the sugar, lemon zest and juice and a tablespoon of water. Cook over a medium heat for about 5 minutes, until you have a moist compote; the softened fruit should be bound in its juices, but with no excess liquid remaining. Remove from the heat and set aside to cool.

Pour the cream into a large bowl and add the vanilla seeds. Add the icing sugar to the cream and whisk until the cream is rich and aerated, but still retains its fluidity (take care not to over whip). Gently fold in the gooseberry compote with a rubber spatula. The finished fool should drop easily off the spatula – it must still be creamy, not a stiff, set mousse.

To serve, cut each greengage half into 3 wedges. Lift the nectarines out of the syrup and chop them into 1cm pieces. Divide the chopped nectarines equally among the glasses containing the gooseberry jelly and divide all but 2 tablespoons of the almond crumble among the glasses.

Cover the crumble with a layer of gooseberry fool. Dress the sliced greengages in a little of the nectarine syrup, put them on top of the fool and finish with a fine sprinkle of the remaining crumble.

Tip: Removing the skin from nectarines can be a tricky process, but if you start with a large, ripe fruit, poach it correctly and allow it to cool in the syrup, all should go well. Use green gooseberries, if possible. The late summer red gooseberries have a higher sugar content, which works less successfully with the cream.

Desserts

White chocolate, bourbon and raspberry cheesecake with raspberry sauce

James Martin

This easy baked cheesecake is melt-in-your-mouth smooth, with an added kick from the vanilla-scented bourbon and the tartness of fresh raspberries.

Preheat the oven to 180°C/350°F/Gas 4. Lightly grease the cake tin.

Place 200g of the white chocolate and the double cream into a bowl suspended over a pan of simmering water (do not let the bottom of the bowl touch the water) and heat until just melted.

Place the sponge disc in the base of the tin. Sprinkle with a little bourbon, if you like.

Place the cream cheese into another bowl and add the vanilla extract. Then beat together with the lemon zest and juice, the bourbon and egg yolks. Stir in the sugar, cornflour and white chocolate cream and mix until thoroughly combined.

Carefully fold in the raspberries and the remaining chopped white chocolate.

Whisk the egg whites until stiff peaks form when the whisk is removed. Fold the whisked egg whites into the cream cheese mixture with a large metal spoon, making sure they are fully incorporated, then pour the mixture over the sponge base in the cake tin.

Set the cheesecake on a large sheet of foil and wrap the foil up around the base of the tin to seal the bottom.

Pour 2–3mm warm water into a roasting tray and sit the cake tin in the tray. (This will help create steam during cooking.) Bake for 1 hour until the top is golden-brown, but the middle of the cake still has a slight wobble. Remove from the oven and allow to cool and set completely before removing from the tin.

For the raspberry sauce, place the raspberries, icing sugar and 50ml water into a blender and purée until smooth. Strain the sauce through a fine sieve, pushing it through with a spatula or spoon, into a bowl.

Slice the cheesecake and serve with a drizzle of raspberry sauce and a dusting of icing sugar.

Serves 8

You'll need a 22cm springform tin

300g white chocolate, roughly chopped
350ml double cream
1 x 22cm ready-made sponge (page 225) or shop-bought cake
50ml bourbon, plus extra for sprinkling over the sponge (optional)
750g full-fat soft cream cheese
1½ tsp vanilla extract
2 lemons, zest and juice
3 eggs, separated
200g caster sugar
4 tbsp cornflour
250g raspberries
icing sugar, for dusting

for the raspberry sauce
250g raspberries
2 tbsp icing sugar

Desserts

Pistachio soufflés

Pierre Koffmann

A signature dish from three-Michelin-star Pierre. The soufflés are light as air and delicately flavoured with pistachio (you can buy the paste online, see Stockists page 234). You could easily use the same quantity of ground unsalted pistachios. Although the soufflés are simple to make, they make a spectacular dessert.

Preheat the oven to 210°C/410°F/Gas 7.

Boil the milk with the pistachio paste.

Beat together the whole egg, egg yolk and half of the sugar for 2 minutes, then add the flour and mix for 1 minute. Pour on the milk mixture, transfer to a saucepan and cook for 4 minutes, whisking continuously. Pour the mixture into a bowl, cover with foil and keep in a warm place.

Grease the inside of 6 individual soufflé dishes with the softened butter and coat with grated chocolate.

Beat the egg whites very stiffly, add the remaining sugar and beat until firm. Whisk the pistachio mixture for a few seconds, then add a quarter of the egg whites and whisk vigorously. Add half the remaining egg whites, stirring quickly with a spatula to make sure there are no lumps. Quickly stir in the rest of the egg whites in the same way.

Pour the soufflé mixture into the prepared dishes and bake in the preheated oven for 8–10 minutes.

Tip: Don't be tempted to open the oven while the soufflés are cooking. Watch them grow through the glass and take them out as soon as they've risen and are starting to go golden.

Serves 6

You'll need 6 individual soufflé dishes

100ml milk
50g pistachio paste (page 234)
1 whole egg
1 egg yolk
50g caster sugar
40g plain flour
20g butter, softened
50g grated good-quality chocolate
6 egg whites

Chocolate chestnut yule log

James Martin

Forget Christmas pudding; this year it's all about the yule log! James keeps his simple with a light chocolate sponge and traditional French rich chestnut and mascarpone filling.

Preheat the oven to 180°C/350°F/Gas 4. Lightly grease the Swiss roll tin and line with non-stick baking paper.

Melt the chocolate in a bowl over a pan of simmering water (the bowl must not touch the water). Whisk the egg yolks and sugar together in a large bowl until pale. Stir in the flour until combined, then stir in the melted chocolate.

Meanwhile, whisk the egg whites until stiff peaks form. Use a large metal spoon to gently fold spoonfuls of the egg whites into the chocolate mixture, until just combined, taking care not to overmix.

Carefully spoon the mixture into the prepared tin, spreading evenly to the edges. Bake for 18–20 minutes, until the cake has risen and springs back when a finger is pressed gently into the centre. Remove from the oven and leave to cool for a few minutes.

Place a clean damp tea towel over the cake with a board on top. Flip the whole thing over so the cake is face down on the tea towel. Remove the tin and peel off the paper. Cover with another clean damp tea towel while you make the filling.

Meanwhile, for the filling, carefully mix the chestnut purée, whipped cream and mascarpone until just combined, then fold in the chopped chestnuts.

Lift the tea towel off the sponge. Using a palette knife or spatula, spread the filling over the sponge, leaving a 2cm border free at the edge.

Starting at the longest side of the cake, gently but firmly roll up the sponge, as you would a Swiss roll, using the tea towel as a guide. Keep the first roll fairly tight so that you get a good spiral shape. Transfer the roll onto a serving tray and decorate with a dusting of icing sugar, bark (see tip) and whatever decorations you like.

Tip: To add 'bark', simply melt 150g milk chocolate, 100g dark chocolate and 300ml double cream in a bowl over a pan of simmering water. Stir and allow to cool to room temperature before spreading over the roulade. As the icing cools, you can use the tines of a fork to create a bark effect.

Serves 6–8

You'll need a 23 x 33cm Swiss roll tin

for the sponge
175g dark chocolate, roughly chopped
6 eggs, separated
175g caster sugar
50g plain flour
2–3 tbsp icing sugar, for dusting

for the filling
150g tin sweetened chestnut purée
150ml double cream, lightly whipped
50g mascarpone
75g cooked chestnuts, roughly chopped

Desserts

Make your
own

The techniques in this chapter require a little time. And patience. You can, of course, buy fresh pasta, bread and pastry, instant stocks and curry pastes in your local supermarket. And often shortcuts are what you need. But for those times when you want to cook for the love of it or for the thrill of learning something new, how much more satisfying (and cheaper!) to make your own. Plus, choosing homemade over shop-bought means that you can control how much salt and sugar and exactly what goes into your food. Which means it's the healthier option too.

Homemade drinks

Susy Atkins

Elderflower cordial

Made with the fragrant, creamy white blossoms of the elderflower, here's how you bottle up a little bit of spring. If you prefer the taste of lemons, you can switch the quantities around, so use three lemons and one lime instead.

Put the sugar in a large preserving pan and pour on the hot water, stirring to dissolve. Cool for 20 minutes.

Meanwhile, shake the elderflower heads to remove dust and insects, then wash them gently in cold water. Drain and shake until nearly dry, then snip off all the main stalks, leaving only the flower sprigs. Push these down into the warm sugar syrup and add the citric acid. Stir.

Thinly pare one-third of the peel from the limes and lemon and add to the pan, then slice all the fruit up and add it too. Stir together, cover tightly, and keep in a cool, dark place for 24 hours. Strain through muslin and bottle.

Keeps for up to 1 month in the fridge or several months in the freezer.

Makes 2 litres

1.8kg sugar
1.8 litres very hot water
25 elderflower sprays/heads (use those that are fully open, but not browning)
1 tbsp citric acid
3 unwaxed limes
1 unwaxed lemon

Make your own

Limoncello

Keep your bottles of limoncello in the freezer and serve icy cold shots after dinner, drizzle over ice cream or use as an ingredient in cocktails or puds.

Pare the rind thinly from the lemons, then steep in the vodka for 1 week.

Make a hot sugar syrup with the sugar and 350ml water, add the vodka and lemon rind and keep for a further week before straining off the peel and bottling. Keeps forever.

Makes 1 litre

2 large unwaxed lemons
500ml vodka
375g sugar

Sloe gin

A classic winter drink. If you're lucky, you'll know where to find sloes each autumn, but if the hard, dusty-matt, purple-blue berries prove elusive, look out for the white flowers of the blackthorn in spring. Come late autumn, that's your sloe bush! Make in autumn and it'll be ready for Christmas.

Pick out any bruised or broken sloes. Freeze the berries and defrost again or prick each one to split the hard skins and release the juice.

Divide the berries equally between 2 medium-size Kilner jars and pour half the sugar over each. Fill the jars with gin, seal and shake gently. Turn the bottles every hour or so for the first day, then once a day for a week, then from time to time.

Leave for at least 6 weeks before drinking. Remove the sloes after 3 months, but the finished liqueur will continue to improve for up to a year. Keeps forever.

Makes 700ml

450g sloes
450g sugar
700ml (standard bottle size) gin

Make your own

Seasonal cocktails

Susy Atkins

Be warned! Not all cocktails are food-friendly – quite the opposite in the case of creamy cocktails or ones with very strong or very sweet flavours and many complex ingredients. Simpler fresh and fruity cocktails with streamlined, clean flavours will complement your cooking though. Try these four through the seasons.

SPRING

Blossom and lime

This is pretty dry and floral, fragrant and slightly herbal – try it with white fish, spring green vegetable dishes or leafy salads.

Shake all the ingredients in a cocktail shaker over plenty of ice and strain into a classic martini glass. Garnish with a thin strand of unwaxed lime zest and/or apple blossom petals.

Makes 1

30ml premium gin (preferably the cucumber and floral-scented Hendrick's)
20ml elderflower cordial (page 208)
10ml dry white vermouth
10ml fresh lime juice
unwaxed lime zest and/or apple blossom petals, to garnish

SUMMER

St Clement's martini

The tangy citrus and slight sweetness here goes with fruit salads, juicy prawns, scallops and other seafood, as well as sweet-and-sour dishes.

Shake all the ingredients together in a cocktail shaker over ice and strain into a classic martini glass. Garnish with a tiny sliver of orange.

Makes 1

25ml limoncello (page 209)
25ml plain vodka
10ml fresh lemon juice
10ml fresh orange juice
orange sliver, to garnish

AUTUMN

Manhattan

A classic cocktail, with an autumnal flavour from the smoky, warming depths of the bourbon whiskey and the additional twist here of blackberries. Sip with cured and spicy cold meats like salami and chorizo or serve with rich meat pâtés.

Stir the whiskey, vermouth and bitters over ice in a jug or cocktail shaker. Strain into a martini glass or short tumbler and let the cherry and blackberry bob about on top.

Makes 1

40ml bourbon whiskey
20ml sweet vermouth
2 dashes Angostura bitters
1 maraschino cherry
1 perfect ripe blackberry

Make your own

Sloe gin fizz

This longer cocktail is refreshing at a party, the bubbles are festive, plus the hint of bitter, almondy sloe works with warm, savoury party canapés.

Shake the 2 gins, the lime juice and sugar syrup in a cocktail shaker over ice and strain into a tall tumbler. Top up with cold sparkling water and sip straightaway.

Makes 1

25ml gin
25ml sloe gin (see page 209 or use a shop-bought brand like Sipsmith's)
15ml fresh lime juice
10ml sugar syrup
150ml chilled sparkling water

Make your own

Stocks and brine

Vegetable stock
James Martin

Just throw some vegetables in a pot and boil. You can, of course, tweak the recipe, depending on your taste and what ingredients you have to hand.

Place all the ingredients in a pan along with 1.2 litres cold water, bring to the boil and simmer for around half an hour. Strain the stock through a sieve, discarding the vegetables.

Once cool, this will keep in the fridge for up to 4 days or freeze in batches for future use.

Makes 750ml

2 carrots, roughly chopped
1 onion, quartered
1 leek, roughly chopped
½ fennel bulb, roughly chopped
2 sticks celery, roughly chopped
2 tomatoes
3 garlic cloves, left whole, gently crushed
½ tsp black peppercorns
1 bay leaf
3 parsley stalks

Fish stock
Nathan Outlaw

Using non-oily white fish bones – ideally turbot or lemon sole – results in a clear, clean stock. Ask your fishmonger for these and use the head, which has a lot of flavour.

Remove the eyes and gills from the head and any guts from the fish bones. Give both a rinse under some cold running water for 10 minutes. Put the bones in a large pan and cover with 2–4 litres cold water.

Turn on to a high heat and bring to the boil, then turn down the heat and allow the stock to just simmer for 20 minutes, skimming off the layer of fat from the top every 5 minutes. Remove the stock from the heat, and allow to cool with the fish bones still inside.

When the stock is at room temperature, pass it through a fine sieve and then again through muslin, then refrigerate. This will keep for 3 days in the fridge, or 2–3 months in the freezer.

Makes 1.5–3 litres

1–2kg non-oily white fish bones

Make your own

Crab stock

Nathan Outlaw

You can use every part of the crab, or just the leftover shells, to make this rich stock. Take care not to let it boil – a gentle simmer is all you need.

Heat the butter in a pot until foaming. Add the whole crabs (or shells), onions, carrots, sliced fennel and fronds, garlic and tomato and fry for 4–5 minutes, or until the vegetables have softened.

Pour in the cider and 2 litres water, then bring the mixture to a simmer and cook for 1 hour. Strain the stock through a sieve set over a saucepan and discard the solids.

Bring the stock to the boil and boil hard for 10 minutes, or until the volume of liquid has reduced by half. Remove the pan from the heat, set aside to cool, then chill.

This will keep for 3 days in the fridge, or 2–3 months in the freezer.

Makes 1.5 litres

50g butter
1kg whole crab (or shells)
2 onions, diced
4 carrots, diced
1 fennel bulb, thinly sliced,
   fronds reserved
1 head garlic, separated into
   cloves, each peeled and
   crushed
10 plum tomatoes,
   de-seeded, chopped
200ml dry cider

Brine

Glynn Purnell

This is a simple, adaptable brine recipe, which you can use for any kind of meat or fish.

Pour a litre of tap water into a large saucepan. Add the salt, sugar, peppercorns, cloves, bay leaf and thyme. Bring to a boil, remove from the heat and set aside to cool.

Add the meat or fish you want to brine, making sure it is fully submerged, cover and leave to soak in the fridge for up to 24 hours.

After brining, rinse the meat or fish to remove any excess salt before cooking.

Makes 750ml

200g coarse sea salt
150g demerara sugar
1 tbsp black peppercorns
2 cloves
1 bay leaf
1 sprig thyme

Make your own

Chicken stock

James Martin

Cheap and nourishing, and as simple as throwing the leftovers from your roast into a big pan, along with any root vegetables or herbs you have. For a cleaner-tasting 'white' stock, use a raw chicken carcass.

Put all the ingredients into a large pan and pour in enough cold water to cover the chicken, about 2.5 litres. Bring to the boil and skim off any scum that has formed on the surface with a ladle or large spoon.

Cover and simmer very gently for 2–2½ hours, skimming as necessary, then strain the stock through a sieve, discarding the vegetables and chicken bones.

Allow to cool, then refrigerate. You can store in the fridge for about 4 days or in the freezer for 2–3 months.

Makes 2 litres

1 roast chicken carcass, with leftover chicken attached
1 carrot, chopped into large pieces
1 onion, quartered
1 stick celery, roughly chopped
6 black peppercorns
1 bay leaf
3 parsley stalks
1 sprig thyme

Sauces and dressings

Basic vinaigrette

Henry Dimbleby

This basic dressing is all you need to dress up a simple mixed leaf or lettuce salad. The recipe is endlessly adaptable, which means you can tweak with any oils, vinegars, herbs and spices you like.

Put all the ingredients into a jar, screw the lid on tightly and shake until you have an emulsion. Adjust the seasoning, lemon juice or olive oil to suit your taste. Store in the fridge.

Makes 150ml

90ml olive oil
2 tbsp white wine vinegar
2 tsp Dijon mustard
2 lemons, juiced
sea salt and freshly ground black pepper

Hazelnut vinaigrette

Tom Kitchin

Adds a lovely crunch to salads or roasted veg (see page 126).

Make the dressing by combining the chopped hazelnuts, shallots, chives and hazelnut oil in a bowl. Add a splash of sherry vinegar and season with salt and pepper, to taste. Store in the fridge.

Makes 150ml

100g skinned hazelnuts, roughly chopped
4 shallots, finely chopped
2 tbsp chopped chives
100ml hazelnut oil
2 tsp sherry vinegar, or to taste
sea salt and freshly ground black pepper

Make your own

Thyme vinaigrette

Ben Tish

A vinaigrette that showcases rich, aromatic Moscatel vinegar (made from Spanish muscat grapes), with its sweet, fruity, persistent flavours. Use to dress crunchy salads, roasted fish or vegetable dishes.

Whisk together the rapeseed oil and the vinegar in a small bowl, season well and then stir in the thyme leaves, lemon juice and Dijon mustard. Store in the fridge.

Makes 150ml

100ml rapeseed oil
5 tbsp Moscatel vinegar (or white balsamic vinegar)
¼ bunch thyme, leaves removed
1 lemon, juiced
½ tsp Dijon mustard
sea salt and freshly ground black pepper

Speedy mayonnaise

Annabel Langbein

If you've struggled to make mayonnaise using the drip method, Annabel's recipe is the one for you – just whizz up the ingredients and it emulsifies in seconds. You will need a hand, stick or immersion blender and a narrow jug.

Place all the ingredients in a narrow bowl or jug and whizz with a hand-blender. It will thicken at once to create a creamy mayonnaise. Add more vegetable oil if desired to create a thicker mayo or a little hot water to give a thinner consistency.

Speedy mayo will keep for up to 2 weeks in a jar in the fridge.

Makes 300g

2 eggs
3 tbsp lemon juice
1 tsp Dijon mustard
½ tsp salt
good pinch white pepper
275ml vegetable oil

Curry mayonnaise

Paul Ainsworth

Great as a dip, with Paul's gourmet Scotch eggs (page 20) or to spice up a couple of ordinary hard-boiled eggs.

To make the curry mayonnaise, place the mayonnaise in a bowl and add the chilli sauce, curry powder and turmeric. Whisk thoroughly and set aside for a few minutes to let the spices penetrate the mayonnaise.

Add the lemon juice and Tabasco, then season to taste with salt and pepper.

Transfer to the fridge to chill until ready to serve.

Makes 125g

100g mayonnaise (preferably homemade)
2 tbsp sweet chilli sauce
2 tsp mild curry powder (such as korma)
½ tsp turmeric
lemon juice, to taste
3 drops Tabasco
sea salt and freshly ground black pepper

Make your own

Quick tomato sauce

Katie Caldesi

Everyone should know how to make a basic tomato sauce and this one is ideal.

Make a cross in the bottom of the tomatoes and blanch in boiling water for 1 minute; remove and refresh in a bowl of ice-cold water. Peel the tomatoes and remove the seeds, then cut them into small dice.

Heat the olive oil in a frying pan and fry the garlic for 1 minute, taking care not to burn it. Season with salt and freshly ground black pepper and add the tomatoes and basil. Cook for a further 5 minutes until the tomatoes have softened, remove the garlic clove and basil and blend in a food processer until smooth.

Serves 4

500g ripe plum tomatoes
2 tbsp extra virgin olive oil
1 garlic clove, finely chopped
1 sprig basil, leaves torn
sea salt and freshly ground
  black pepper

Quick pickled lemons

Ashley Palmer-Watts

Quicker than preserved lemons (ready in hours, rather than weeks), these add a lovely tart flavour to couscous, slow-cooked stews, salads, chicken and fish – in fact just about any Middle Eastern or Mediterranean dish.

Gently heat 150ml water, the vinegar and sugar together in a pan. Once the sugar has dissolved, remove from the heat and allow the mixture to cool completely.

In the meantime, slice the lemons widthways to make circular cross sections, using a mandolin if you have one. Carefully ensure all pips are discarded.

Place the lemons in the cooled pickling liquid. Transfer to a bowl or large jar, cover and place in the fridge for 48 hours before using.

Makes 1 large jar

125ml Chardonnay vinegar
50g golden caster sugar
2 lemons, Amalfi if possible

Make your own

The Indian kitchen

Sprouted fenugreek seeds
Vivek Singh

Fenugreek seeds taste bitter when raw, but when they're germinated, they're a lot more palatable. They are easy to sprout, great in salads, and extremely good for you. Vivek reckons they're the next Indian superfood and it is claimed they help reduce cholesterol, improve skin and digestion, and even control diabetes!

Soak the seeds in water overnight. Drain, then place between 2 pieces of moist kitchen paper in a warm place. Keep the paper moist for a couple of days, until the sprouts have reached about 5cm.

100g fenugreek seeds

Mint chutney
Atul Kochhar

This basic chutney can be used as a dipping sauce or to complement and cool a curry. Spicy, fresh, aromatic, and takes seconds to prepare.

Put all the ingredients except the yoghurt into a food processor and blend until well combined. Add the yoghurt and whisk until well combined. Add salt and freshly ground black pepper to taste, and chill in the fridge until required.

Makes 400g

200g mint leaves
110g coriander leaves
2 tbsp chopped red onion
2 tbsp lemon juice
1 green chilli, chopped finely
½ tsp salt
½ tbsp vegetable oil
5 tbsp Greek yoghurt
sea salt and freshly ground
    black pepper

Madras paste
Lawrence Keogh

Of course you can buy shop-bought, but this is so easy and quick to make. Stirred into coconut milk, it provides a delicious base for a quick week night curry. Or try marinating lamb cutlets in curry paste mixed with natural yoghurt.

Toast the coriander seeds, mustard seeds, cumin seeds, chilli powder and turmeric in a dry frying pan over a medium heat. When they start to pop and crackle in the pan, add the peppercorns and toast for another minute. Remove from the heat and set aside.

Add the garlic and ginger to the spice mix and place in a mini blender or pestle and mortar. Add the vinegar and blitz or pound to a smooth paste.

Store in an airtight container and it will keep for up to a month in the fridge.

Makes 100g

1 tbsp coriander seeds,
    ground
½ tsp brown mustard seeds
1 tbsp cumin seeds, ground
½ tsp chilli powder (such as
    cayenne)
½ tsp turmeric
¼ tsp cracked black
    peppercorns
2 garlic cloves, finely
    chopped
1 tsp grated fresh ginger
75ml white vinegar

Make your Own

Flavoured butters

These flavoured butters are great to have to hand: make a batch and keep it in the fridge for two weeks or in the freezer for a couple of months.

Tarragon and anchovy butter

Nathan Outlaw

Works beautifully with delicate fish dishes or grilled meats.

Put the softened butter into a bowl. Chop the tarragon and add to the butter with the chopped shallots and anchovies. Mix well until evenly combined and season with pepper and a little salt, if needed, to taste.

Shape the butter into a roll on a sheet of cling film, wrap in the film and tie the ends to seal. Refrigerate to firm up.

Makes 200g

200g butter, softened
1 bunch tarragon, leaves only
2 shallots, peeled, finely chopped
4 salted anchovy fillets, chopped
sea salt and freshly ground black pepper

Garlic and parsley butter

Glynn Purnell

Flavour is key, so use a good-quality salted butter. If you don't have wild garlic, simply add an extra clove of ordinary garlic.

Place the parsley, garlic and wild garlic leaves in a blender and blend until smooth. Put the butter in a bowl and beat with a wooden spoon until it is soft and creamy, then mash in the blended parsley and garlic.

Shape the butter into a roll on a sheet of cling film, wrap in the film and tie the ends to seal. Refrigerate to firm up.

Makes 150g

½ bunch flat-leaf parsley
1 garlic clove, chopped
5–6 large wild garlic leaves
150g salted butter, softened

Make your own

Pasta doughs

Rich egg pasta
Theo Randall

Fresh pasta is very easy to make and roll out using a food processor and pasta machine. Traditionally, every region in Italy has different ways of making pasta dough with varying ratios of flour and eggs. Theo uses lots of eggs for a tasty, sunny yellow pasta. 'Try Italian eggs,' he says. 'They have much richer yolks than most of the eggs you can buy in the UK, since the chickens are fed a diet of corn and carrots, which enhances the colour and texture of the yolk.'

To make the pasta, place all the ingredients in a food processor and pulse until they form a yellow ball of dough with a smooth, firm but slightly sticky texture, almost like Plasticine. If it seems wet, add an extra teaspoon or 2 of flour.

Divide the dough into 2 equal balls and immediately wrap them in cling film to prevent drying out. The dough will keep in the fridge for up to 10 days.

With the rollers of your pasta machine on their widest setting, pass a piece of dough through, then fold into 3. Give it a quarter turn and pass it through the machine again. Repeat this 5 or 6 times so the gluten in the pasta is thoroughly worked, then pass it through the machine to roll out, progressively narrowing the rollers by one notch each time. Make this as thin as you feel comfortable with. The more the pasta has been worked initially, the thinner you will be able to roll it. Make sure the pasta sheet is no more than 60cm long, otherwise it will be difficult to handle and it may break. Repeat with the other piece of dough.

Use the cutters on your machine to cut the dough into your favourite shape. Place the cut pasta on a long tray in a single layer, dusting with semolina so it doesn't stick. Cover with greaseproof paper and leave in the fridge overnight. This will help dry out the pasta and give it a better texture once it's cooked.

Tip: If there's no room in your fridge, put the cut pasta on a wire rack and leave to dry at room temperature for 12 hours. The pasta should be firm, but not too brittle; if it's brittle it will break when you pick it up, which is the last thing you want.

Serves 6–8

300g Italian 'oo' flour
100g fine semolina (durum wheat) flour, plus extra for dusting
2 large eggs
6 large egg yolks

Make your own

Fresh egg pasta

Antonio Carluccio

If you've never made fresh pasta before, this is the simplest recipe to start with. Originating in the northern region of Emilia Romagna, the gastronomic heartland of Italy, Carluccio's version uses the basic ratio of 100g flour to 1 egg, mixed with a pinch of salt. You can experiment using different flours, but Italian 'oo' flour is the easiest to work by hand and gives the dough a smooth, silky texture.

Sift the flour onto a work surface, forming it into a volcano-shaped mound with a well in the centre. Break the eggs into the well and add the salt. Incorporate the eggs into the flour with a fork and your hands, gradually drawing the flour into the egg mixture until it forms a coarse paste.

Add a little more flour if the mixture is too soft or sticky – or a little water if the mixture is too dry. Using your knife (or a spatula), scrape up any stray pieces of dough.

Before kneading the dough, clean your hands and the work surface. Lightly flour the work surface, and start to knead the dough with the heel of one hand. Work the dough for 10–15 minutes until the consistency is smooth and elastic. If you have dough sticking to your fingers, rub your hands with some flour. Wrap the dough in clingfilm or foil and leave it to rest for at least half an hour.

Lightly flour your work surface and a rolling pin. Gently roll out the dough, working from the middle and rolling away from you, rotating the dough in quarter turns. As you roll, stretch the dough with the rolling pin. Turn the dough over every now and then to keep it an even thickness. Keep the work surface and rolling pin well floured to prevent sticking.

Alternatively, you can use a pasta machine to 'knead' the dough. Simply divide the dough into manageable pieces (according to the machine's instructions). Roll a piece of dough through the steel rollers with a maximum gap of about 1cm. Repeat with the same piece of dough, each time reducing the size of the gap, until the desired thickness is reached. Being forced through a smaller gap, the pasta dough is worked more, becoming thinner and more silky.

If you are making filled pasta, go straight ahead and incorporate the filling as in the recipes. If you are making flat pasta or shapes, leave the pasta on a clean tea towel to dry for about half an hour before cutting. Coil long pasta into nests as this will make it easier to handle when you come to cook it.

Serves 6

400g Italian 'oo' flour, plus
  extra for dusting
4 medium eggs
pinch salt

Make your own

Pastry and baking

Sweet pastry
Richard Bertinet

Pastry freezes very well for a limited time – about two months. Richard advises you to wrap fresh pastry in greaseproof paper, then place in a bag. You can also freeze blind-baked pastry cases.

Put the softened butter into a bowl with the flour and salt and tear it into pieces. Try to keep the butter completely coated with flour at all times so it doesn't stick.

Gently flake the butter into the flour as if you are dealing a pack of cards. Stop flaking when the pieces of butter are the size of your little fingernail. Tip the sugar, eggs and extra yolk into the flour and mix everything together.

Work the dough in the bowl by pressing down with both thumbs, turning the bowl a quarter turn and repeating a few times. Turn the dough out and work and turn it a few more times.

Fold the dough over onto itself and press it down with your fingertips. Repeat this process until the dough is like Plasticine and looks homogenous.

Shape the dough into a square by tapping the edges on the work surface so you start with a neat shape, rather than rough edges.

Rest in the fridge for at least 1 hour – preferably several – or, better still, overnight.

Tip: Richard uses cold butter straight from the fridge. Transform very hard butter into something soft and pliable by putting the butter between 2 pieces of greaseproof paper and bashing it firmly with a rolling pin until it is 1cm thick.

Makes enough for one 20cm tart or 12 tartlets

125g unsalted butter, bashed
  (see tip)
350g plain flour
pinch salt
125g caster sugar
2 medium eggs
1 egg yolk

Make your own

Génoise sponge

James Martin

This plainest of bakes is light and springy, making it the perfect texture for creating sandwich cakes, for rolling into Swiss rolls or yule logs, layering up or swirling with lashings of cream, chocolate and fresh fruit.

Preheat the oven to 180°C/350°F/Gas 4. Grease and line the cake tin.

Place the sugar and eggs in a large bowl and beat with a hand mixer for about 10 minutes until it is pale, doubles in volume and holds a thick ribbon when dripped from the whisk.

Fold in the flour and warm melted butter and pour into the prepared cake tin.

Bake in the oven for 20–30 minutes, or until the cake has risen and is springy to the touch. Remove from the oven and set aside to cool. When cool enough to handle, turn out onto a wire rack to cool completely.

Makes 1 cake

You'll need a 22cm round cake tin

125g caster sugar
4 medium eggs, at room
   temperature
125g plain flour
25g butter, just melted

Make your own

Pâte brisée (shortcrust pastry)

Stéphane Reynaud

A rich, buttery pastry, ideal for both sweet and savoury pies, as well as tarts and quiches. Wrapped in cling film or greaseproof paper and a bag, it can be stored in the fridge for several days or frozen for about a month.

Cut the butter into cubes and leave to soften slightly.

Combine the flour and salt on a work surface, add the butter and work the dough with your fingertips until the mixture resembles breadcrumbs.

Make a well in the mixture, place the egg yolks and water in the centre and mix using one hand, starting from the centre of the well.

Bring the dough together into a smooth ball.

Let it rest in the refrigerator, covered in cling film, for 30 minutes before using.

Makes about 875g pastry

250g butter, chilled
500g good-quality plain flour
2 scant teaspoons salt
2 egg yolks
100ml ice-cold water

Easy flatbreads

Angela Hartnett

This is the easiest bread you'll ever make, with quick rise yeast and a food processor to do the kneading. Pair with grilled meat or your favourite curry.

Place the flour and salt in a stand mixer with a dough hook attachment and dissolve the yeast and sugar in the water.

Add the oil to the flour and salt along with the yeast mixture and mix with the dough hook. Knead for 5 minutes, then tip the dough into a bowl, cover loosely and prove for about an hour until doubled in size.

Heat a cast-iron pan and divide the dough into balls. Roll out and cook for a couple of minutes on each side until the bread has bubbled and is crisp and coloured.

Makes 12–15 flatbreads

500g strong bread flour
1 tsp salt
10g instant yeast
pinch sugar
300ml warm water
2 tsp olive oil

Make your own

Olive oil bread

Michel Roux Jr

This simple white bread is similar to a baguette and is great for sandwiches.
It also makes good croutons as it crisps up well in the oven.

Dissolve the yeast in the warm water, add the flour and knead for 15 minutes until silky and elastic. Add the olive oil and fine salt, then knead again for 5 minutes. Cover the dough and leave it to rise for 40 minutes.

Knock back the dough and form it into a long loaf. Place this on a non-stick baking sheet, cover and leave to rise for another 20 minutes.

Preheat the oven to 220°C/425°F/Gas 7.

Lightly brush the top of the loaf with milk and add a sprinkling of coarse sea salt, then place it in the oven and bake for 30 minutes or until cooked through. Cool on a wire rack.

Makes 1 loaf

12g fresh yeast
275ml warm water
500g stoneground strong
    unbleached bread flour
4 tbsp olive oil
1 heaped tsp fine salt
milk, for brushing
pinch coarse sea salt

Make your own

What to drink

Susy Atkins

Good news – most wine goes reasonably well with most food. Sure, there's the odd terrible clash but in general any wine you like goes with any food you like. But here's the thing – when exactly the right wine is chosen to marry with a particular recipe, the results can be utterly beguiling, enhancing both drink and dish, raising them both up a notch, almost magically. Who wouldn't want to achieve that, especially when we are cooking at our very best?

So here are a few of my tips on picking the right wine.

Don't overwhelm

Rich food needs rich wine, so roll out a full-bodied, tannic red like a southern French Minervois or Aussie Shiraz for roast lamb, char-grilled steak or full-flavoured hard cheese, but equally stick to lighter, simpler, fresher styles like Beaujolais or Chilean Pinot Noir for, say, cold meat salads. Same goes for whites: oaky, juicy Chardonnay suits seafood in buttery, creamy sauces, but crisp, citrussy Sauvignon or Rieslings are better for plain grilled white fish. Aim for a good balance, not a contrast in weight.

Think saucy

If a dish suits a squeeze of lemon (e.g. salad leaves or fish), go for a lemony white wine with it; or if the meat goes with redcurrant sauce, crack open a red wine with red-berry flavours. Peppery Shiraz suits peppered meats, spicy Carmenere from Chile goes with Indian curries, and appley white wines like Chenin Blanc suit pork with apple sauce. It really can be that easy.

Think about all the flavours on the plate

Complex dishes will have 'stand-out' ingredients to match with wine – spice, perhaps, or a rich sauce or gravy, or herbs. Match those, not just a main ingredient, which may not be particularly strongly flavoured (turkey is the classic example of this – match the stuffing, side dishes and gravy, not the blander meat).

Sweetness/dryness counts for a lot

Savoury dishes need dry, or dryish, wines so never bring out a honeyed sparkler like Asti with savoury, salty party snacks. Serve a 'brut' sparkler or dry still wines instead. But always pour luscious dessert wines with anything remotely sweet. Even fresh fruit needs a semi-sweet style with it, and chocolate can take something very sugary indeed.

What to drink

Think seasonal

In general, certain wine styles suit certain seasons. In the spring and summer serve rosés and dry, unoaked whites (always cold) and lighter, tangier reds (perhaps lightly chilled) with simple green vegetable dishes, salads, plainer fish and seafood and lighter meat dishes. In the colder months bring out richer, oakier whites, and more savoury, heavier, more tannic reds with slow braised stews, roasts, pasta bakes, spicy curries.

Here are some of my favourite wine and food matches through the seasons.

Spring

Asparagus with cool, grassy, zingy New Zealand Sauvignon Blanc.

Spring lamb with youthful, strawberry-scented Spanish Tempranillo.

Summer

Strawberries with ice-cold sparkling sweet Moscato.

Sardines with light, crisp Portuguese Vinho Verde.

Autumn

Cooked apples or pears with sweet, but fresh, appley dessert Riesling.

Sausages and mash or sausage casseroles with mellow, soft and peppery Rhône reds.

Winter

Roast pork or porchetta with rich Chenin Blanc or white Burgundy.

Roast pheasant with medium-bodied, cherryish Chianti Classico.

what to drink

What's in season

Cooking seasonally means getting to enjoy the best, local ingredients, bursting with flavour. Don't always deny yourself the exotic, but for everyday exciting suppers, let these quick reference guides inspire you with some great British treats.

Fruit

	Jan	Feb	Mar	Apr	May	Jun	Jul	Aug	Sept	Oct	Nov	Dec
Apples	●								●	●	●	●
Apricots					●	●	●	●				
Blackberries							●	●	●	●		
Blueberries							●	●	●			
Bramley apples	●	●	●									●
Cherries						●	●	●				
Damsons									●	●		
Gooseberries					●	●	●	●				
Greengages					●	●	●	●				
Lemons	●	●	●									
Nectarines							●	●	●	●		
Peaches							●	●	●	●		
Pears	●									●	●	●
Plums								●	●	●		
Raspberries								●	●			
Redcurrants							●	●	●			
Strawberries						●	●	●	●			
Tomatoes							●	●	●	●		

What's in season

Meat and game

	Jan	Feb	Mar	Apr	May	Jun	Jul	Aug	Sept	Oct	Nov	Dec
Goose	●								●	●	●	●
Grouse								●	●	●	●	●
Lamb				●	●	●	●	●	●	●	●	
Partridge	●								●	●	●	●
Pheasant	●										●	●
Rabbit	●	●	●	●	●	●	●	●	●	●	●	●
Venison	●	●									●	●
Woodcock	●										●	●

Wild plants

	Jan	Feb	Mar	Apr	May	Jun	Jul	Aug	Sept	Oct	Nov	Dec
Borage flowers						●	●	●	●			
Ceps (porcini)							●	●	●	●	●	
Chestnuts	●									●	●	●
Chives		●	●	●								
Dandelions				●	●							
Elderflowers				●	●	●						
Hazelnuts								●	●	●		
Horseradish						●	●	●	●	●	●	
Morels			●	●	●							
Samphire							●	●				
Sloes									●	●	●	
Summer truffles								●	●	●	●	●
Walnuts									●	●	●	
Watercress			●	●	●				●	●		
Wild garlic			●	●	●							
Wild rocket			●	●	●	●						

What's in season

Vegetables

	Jan	Feb	Mar	Apr	May	Jun	Jul	Aug	Sept	Oct	Nov	Dec
Artichokes (Jerusalem)	●	●									●	●
Artichokes (globe)					●	●	●	●	●	●		
Artichokes (mammole)		●	●	●	●							
Asparagus					●	●						
Aubergines							●	●	●	●		
Beetroot	●	●				●	●	●	●	●	●	●
Broad beans					●	●	●	●				
Broccoli (Calabrese)						●	●	●	●	●	●	
Brussels sprouts	●	●									●	●
Butternut squash									●	●	●	●
Cabbages	●	●								●	●	●
Cauliflower				●	●	●	●	●	●	●	●	●
Celeriac	●	●	●							●	●	●
Chard	●							●	●	●	●	●
Chicory	●	●	●							●	●	●
Courgettes							●	●	●	●		
Endive	●	●									●	●
Fennel						●	●	●	●	●		
French beans						●	●	●	●	●		
Garlic					●	●	●	●				
Jersey Royals				●	●							
Leeks	●	●	●							●	●	●
Lettuce				●	●	●	●	●	●			
Onions	●	●					●	●	●	●	●	●
Parsnips	●	●								●	●	●
Peas				●	●	●	●	●	●			
Peppers/chillies								●	●	●	●	

Vegetables (cont.)

	Jan	Feb	Mar	Apr	May	Jun	Jul	Aug	Sept	Oct	Nov	Dec
Pumpkin								●	●	●	●	●
Radishes				●	●	●	●	●				
Rhubarb	●	●	●	●	●	●	●					
Romanesco							●	●	●	●	●	●
Runner beans							●	●	●	●		
Spinach						●	●	●	●	●	●	
Sweetcorn								●	●	●		

Fish

	Jan	Feb	Mar	Apr	May	Jun	Jul	Aug	Sept	Oct	Nov	Dec
Cod	●	●								●	●	●
Crab				●	●	●	●	●	●	●		
Cuttlefish					●	●	●	●				
Haddock	●	●				●	●	●	●	●	●	●
Lobster						●	●	●	●	●	●	
Mackerel						●	●	●	●	●	●	
Mussels	●	●	●							●	●	
Oysters	●	●	●							●	●	●
Plaice	●				●	●	●	●	●	●	●	●
Pollock			●	●	●	●	●	●	●	●	●	●
Prawns	●	●	●	●	●	●	●	●				●
Salmon (wild)			●	●	●	●			●	●		
Sardines						●	●	●	●			
Scallops							●	●	●	●		
Sea bass						●	●	●	●	●	●	
Squid								●	●	●	●	
Whiting	●	●									●	●

What's in season

Stockists

Buying seasonal British produce will make all the difference to your cooking and if you're shopping in the right places – your local butcher, greengrocer, fishmonger or farmers' market – you're off to a good start. For any hard-to-source ingredients, online shopping is ideal. Here are some stockists to get you started.

The Asian Cookshop has an excellent range of Indian, Chinese, Thai and Japanese ingredients.
www.theasiancookshop.co.uk

Brindisa for a range of top-quality, hard-to-find Spanish food, including beautiful hams and cheeses, pimentón and saffron, and much more.
www.brindisa.com

First Leaf supply mixed punnets of seasonal, edible flowers, available from March to September.
www.firstleaf.co.uk

Fine Food Specialist for delicious, seasonal items such as truffles, British lamb, English asparagus, wild garlic, candy beetroot and more.
www.finefoodspecialist.co.uk

La Fromagerie has a great online 'cheese room' where you can search by animal and country of origin.
www.lafromagerie.co.uk

Mex Grocer stocks authentic corn tortillas (or a tortilla press and masa harina flour for making your own tortillas), alongside an impressive range of Latin American canned goods, herbs and spices.
www.mexgrocer.co.uk

Mount Fuji for when you're cooking Japanese: the range includes sushi starter kits, noodles, miso soups, rice crackers, Japanese beer, sake and plum wine.
www.mountfuji.co.uk

Sous Chef stocks all the ingredients an adventurous home cook will ever need in the kitchen, plus a treasure trove of specialist equipment and technical information.
www.souschef.co.uk

The Spicery is a fantastic resource for chillies, spices and aromatic blends. You can buy ingredients in any size, from just a teaspoon upwards.
www.thespicery.com

Steenbergs Organic is an award-winning site for good-quality and ethically sourced spices, seasonings, tea, coffee and other grocery items.
www.steenbergs.co.uk

Natoora stocks the freshest European seasonal vegetables and wonderful charcuterie.
www.natoora.co.uk

Pure Spain for hard-to-find Spanish produce: everything from wood-roasted piquillo peppers to chorizo, tapenade and cheese.
www.purespain.co.uk

Spices of India is a one-stop shop for pickles, chutneys, pastes and spices. Buy spices in the smallest possible quantities because they are fragile and don't keep well.
www.spicesofindia.co.uk

Thai Food Online for all things Thai.
www.thai-food-online.co.uk

Turkish Supermarket for authentic Turkish produce, from olives to beer to Turkish delight.
www.turkishsupermarket.co.uk

Why Nut for pistachio and other nut pastes.
www.whynut.co.uk

Main contributors

Chef patron of the two-Michelin-starred pub The Hand and Flowers, Tom Kerridge published his first book, *Proper Pub Food* with an accompanying BBC TV series in 2013.

James Martin opened his first restaurant aged 21, and started his TV career on *Ready Steady Cook*, aged 24. The author of numerous best-selling books (most recently *Fast Cooking*), he has presented *Saturday Kitchen* for the past eight years.

'Greedy Italian' and bestselling author Gennaro Contaldo is widely known as the man who taught Jamie Oliver all he knows about Italian cooking.

Angela Hartnett is Chef Proprietor at Michelin-starred Murano in Mayfair, Proprietor at Café Murano in St James and co-founder of Merchants Tavern in Shoreditch. Angela is also the author of *Cucina* and *Angela's Kitchen*.

Scotland's hottest Michelin-starred chef, Tom Kitchin is author of *Kitchin Suppers* and *From Nature to Plate*, and chef patron of The Kitchin in Edinburgh.

Bryn Williams is the chef patron of Odette's and author of *For the Love of Veg* and *Bryn's Kitchen*.

Phil Howard is head chef and co-owner of the Michelin-starred restaurant The Square in London, and author of *The Square Volume 1*, *Savoury* and *Volume 2*, *Sweet*.

Saturday Kitchen wine expert Susy Atkins is a columnist for the *Sunday Telegraph's Stella* magazine and drinks editor at *Delicious*. Her most recent book is the award-winning *How to Make Your Own Drinks*.

Index

Index

Cactus have produced *Saturday Kitchen* for over eight years, the last two from our purpose-built studio complex, complete with its own cookery school run with Michel Roux Jr. It's an amazing privilege for a foodie like me to meet and work with the best chefs in the world. The production is executed on a low budget, by a small team of dedicated professionals who do us proud. The considerable efforts of the following people make it a quality show that's great fun to work on. Our warmest thanks go to:

The core production team: James Winter, Andy Clarke, Charlotte Johnstone, Hannah Wilson, Claire Paine, James Ross, Chris Worthington, Lizzie Search, Jo Birkinshaw, Will Learmonth, and all the other Cactus staff who work on the show, including Maureen McPhee and all the enthusiastic runners.

The food team: Michaela Bowles, Alan Thatcher, Katie and Dave.

Prolink Television Facilities: the Dugards and all our fabulous crew, especially Silvana, Jeremy, Naomi, Ben, Guy, Rob, Steve, Martin, Neil and the gang; 'Lofty', Toby, Murray and Tom on cameras. Our studio directors, Geri, Dino and Toby. Cheers to Mike and Ben for the wine shoots and honorary crew member, the lovely Louise, for being there.

Everyone at the BBC for their support: Damian Kavanagh, James Dundas, but especially Carla-Maria Lawson our commissioning executive who has to watch over everything we do – here's to the next two years!

Orion for producing another great book we can be proud of. Camilla Howarth for pulling the Cactus contribution together and Dave Skinner for constant support.

James Martin for hosting, along with Tom Kerridge, Angela Hartnett and Matt Tebbutt; our brilliant wine experts Susie Barrie, Susy Atkins, Olly Smith, Peter Richards, Jane Parkinson, Tim Atkin and, of course, all the amazing chefs from all over the world whose performances make the show so special.

And finally Simon and my beautiful sons for letting me ruin their weekends.

Amanda Ross

Amanda Ross, Executive Producer of *Saturday Kitchen* and co-founder of Cactus with her husband Simon

Acknowledgements